THE
ENGLISH
SPIRIT

THE ENGLISH SPIRIT

The Little Gidding
Anthology of English Spirituality

compiled by
Paul Handley, Fiona MacMath,
Pat Saunders and Robert Van de Weyer

Darton, Longman and Todd
London
Published in association with
Little Gidding books

First published in 1987 by
Darton, Longman and Todd Ltd
89 Lillie Road, London SW6 1UD

in association with
Little Gidding Books
Little Gidding, Huntingdon PE17 5RJ

Reprinted 1988

Introductions and selection © 1987 Little Gidding Books

ISBN 0 232 51741 X (Cased)
ISBN 0 232 51767 3 (Paperback)

British Library Cataloguing in Publication Data

The English spirit : the Little Gidding
  anthology of English spirituality.
  1. English literature 2. Christianity—
Literary collections
I. Handley, Paul
820.8′0382   PR1111.C52/

ISBN 0–232–51741–X
ISBN 0–232–51767–3 Pbk

Phototypeset by Input Typesetting Ltd, London SW19 8DR
Printed and bound in Great Britain by
Anchor Brendon Ltd, Tiptree, Essex

Introduction

'O God, if there be a God, save my soul, if I have a soul!'
Prayer of a common soldier before the battle of Blenheim
(quoted in Newman's *Apologia*)

The English have never been quite at ease with the spiritual side of their nature. At times it rises to the surface and they talk (but more commonly write) about their views of God or the spiritual world or, at the very least, the non-material part of themselves. Usually, though, they are uncomfortable with such public soul-searching and concentrate on what they think of as decidedly non-spiritual subjects, like politics and, well, religion.

Even this is an over-simplification. During the times of popular spiritual awareness, such as the fourteenth and seventeenth centuries, the English have been deeply suspicious of anything which strays from 'normal' religion into what they regard as excess. The reclusive Julian of Norwich was perfectly acceptable while the rowdy Margery Kempe was tried for heresy; Jeremy Taylor was made a bishop while George Fox was imprisoned and constantly pilloried for such things as refusing to doff his hat.

Meanwhile, during more materialistic times, such as the late sixteenth century, the early nineteenth and most of the twentieth century, this spiritual nature is never far below the surface, governing personal behaviour and emerging in unconscious moral decisions.

Whether they like it or not, no one simply conjures up this 'higher sense'. Just as the language we use has been developed by generations of English speakers (and before that by Latin, French and Saxon speakers), so our moral sense, our spiritual sense, our sense of God – or whatever we call it – has been shaped by the people around us and before us.

This, then, is the claim being made in these pages, if an anthology can do such a thing as make a claim: that the pieces collected here have played a major part in forming the English character, the English spirit.

These are not obscure writings by marginal ecclesiastics. The people represented here have held a central place on the public stage, in politics, at court, in literature and in the Church (which was considerably more influential in the past). Their works have been read, prayed, sung and pondered on by a far greater proportion of the population than have the more standard works of literature. More people have sung a Wesley hymn than have seen a live performance of Shakespeare, for example.

Definition

'Spirituality is the basis and foundation of human life . . . It must underlie everything. To put it briefly, man is a spiritual being, and the proper work of his mind is to interpret the world according to his higher nature, and to conquer the material aspects of the world so as to bring them into subjection to the spirit.'

Robert Bridges, from the introduction to *The Spirit of Man*

A definition might be helpful at this stage. The word 'spirituality' seems daunting but is perfectly straightforward. It is simply the way someone *does* their religion – not what they believe but what they do with what they believe.

The word is commonly applied to the way someone does their prayers, the way they worship, their meditations, and so on, rather as a modern alternative to the words 'piety' and 'devotion'. But this is to limit the true scope of the word and miss out on the aspect of it which is most central to the way the *English* do their religion: the spirituality of everyday, the influence religion has on the way people work, sleep and have babies.

In some ways spirituality might seem less important than other aspects of religion, like doctrine, for instance. On the other hand, since it is the more practical side of religion, it is also the more visible. Although people were questioned about their beliefs during the Reformation and the English Civil War, most of the contention was caused by spiritual *behaviour*. Roman Catholic doctrine might well have been disputed, but it was non-attendance at the parish church which provoked the most criticism and was punished by the recusancy laws.

In addition, St Paul in his first letter to Timothy sets personal holiness and moral uprightness as the two chief requirements of any church official (not, as is usually the case today, administrative prowess and a capacity for flannel).

Moreover, unlike belief, spirituality is not the domain of the firmly religious. Rather it is felt and practised in some way by people with just the vaguest sense of a 'something beyond-ness' about their world.

The English

'We went to every house in the place, and found each a scene of the greatest ignorance and vice. We saw but one Bible in all the parish, and that was used to prop a flower-pot!'   Hannah More, in a letter to Mr Wilberforce

So this English spirit – what is it composed of?

First of all, it has to be recognised that it is almost entirely *Christian*. Even with the agnostics represented in this book, is it too glib to say that it's the Christian God which they don't believe in? English humanism is in general built on behaviour and morality derived from Christian sources.

The most important and recurring element is *moderation*. Time and again the excesses of Continental religious movements have been held off with Canute-like stubbornness and phlegm, though occasionally at some cost.

During the Middle Ages the prevalent intellectual scholasticism was tempered by an appreciation of the comfortable, homely side of Christ; later on, when the

3

interest in the suffering Christ and his mother grew into a full-blown love affair, it was held in check by a common-sensical scepticism. The English Reformation was master-minded by a moderate scholar with a love of the past rather than by a radical reformer. The new religious movements of the seventeenth and eighteenth centuries, despite the antagonism which they provoked, were attempts to restore forgotten aspects of Christianity to what was considered an unbalanced Church. In the present day, what the High Church and Low Church factions in the Church of England see as opposing views are regarded as complementary by the vast majority of worshippers travelling the *via media*.

Whenever a new religious movement is taken on board the English ship, a number of the existing passengers rush across and hang over the other side in order to offset its weight. What keeps the ship on an even keel, however (albeit with occasionally violent rocking), is not these but the solid ballast in the middle which greets any new development with scepticism and is ready to ridicule its excesses.

This is reflected in part in the language. So 'piety' is acceptable, but not when it turns into 'pietism'; 'religion' itself is all right, but beware of 'religiosity'.

This phlegmatic moderation is both the English strength and the English weakness. Although they balance on a knife-edge between excessive zeal and unbelief, it is the broad, blunt edge of the blade and really not such an uncomfortable place to sit. The English find it remarkably easy to resist enthusiasm, whereas this lumpen inertia constantly threatens to overwhelm any spiritual sense they might have.

It would be wrong, however, to conclude that the English never make any spiritual efforts. To move in one direction then to counterbalance it, to feel enthusiasm then to curb it, is not the same as not moving, not feeling. The Thirty-nine Articles is a case in point. The clear-headed Calvinistic zeal with which they were drawn up was sincerely felt; just as sincere, though, is the sheepish disre-gard the Church of England has had for them ever since.

The combination of the two is quintessentially English.

Beyond this, the English spirit is essentially *practical*. Any spiritual impulse, in order to take root in the English character, has to be grounded in everyday life. This is one reason for the English suspicion of monasteries and other religious houses and their brand of spirituality which cannot be followed by ordinary people.

It is *domestic*. At one level this means that for generations English piety has been practised in the home. But it also gives a flavour to the English brand of Christianity where family and homely images are constantly in use.

It has a strong *lay* bias. The Puritan Reformation merely confirmed the suspicion of the priesthood which had grown up during the Middle Ages. The Catholic priest-hood has never recovered from the blow to its prestige delivered during the recusant years, when the priests were employed and protected by powerful lay families. In general, those with spiritual influence are more likely to be secular than clerical.

It is *optimistic*. Both the purgatorial, hell-fire Catholicism and the harsh, judgemental Calvinism have been kept at arm's length in favour of a fundamentally happy view of Christianity. Dame Julian's often quoted conclusion: 'All shall be well and all shall be well and all manner of thing shall be well' finds resonances throughout English spiritual writing.

It is many other things as well: the English are never happy to stray too far from Scripture; they tend not to use their imaginations; their devotions are centred on Christ; they are uneasy about the Holy Spirit. These characteristics are not of course to be seen in every writer; nor are they exclusive to the English. Taken together and as a whole, however, they do form a distinct English tradition.

Little Gidding

'There are other places
Which also are at the world's end. . .
But this is the nearest, in place and time,
Now and in England.'

T. S. Eliot, from 'Little Gidding', *Four Quartets*

This is not subtitled 'The Little Gidding Book of English Spirituality' just because the four compilers live in the ecumenical community there. Regardless of that, Little Gidding has a central place in English spirituality, and in its history can be traced many of the elements listed above.

In 1626 Nicholas Ferrar, at the age of 34, gave up a promising political career and bought the neglected manor house at Little Gidding in Huntingdonshire. Together with his mother, his brother and sister and their families, he established a lay religious community and observed a simple rule of prayer, the whole household processing from the manor house to the church three times a day. They practised various crafts, including tapestry and the bookbinding which brought them to King Charles I's attention.

The poet George Herbert was made prebend in the neighbouring village of Leighton Bromswold, and Nicholas Ferrar helped plan and supervise the restoration of Herbert's church. The Community ran a school and a small dispensary for local families and their children and attracted a good deal of interest, not all of it sympathetic, from travellers on the Great North Road nearby.

A distinguishing feature of the Little Gidding Community was its willingness to blend elements from different church traditions at a time when the Church in England was polarising. Rigorous Puritan simplicity was combined with Catholic ritual and the Community's religious neutrality was guarded carefully.

Ironically, though, the Community fell victim to that other English characteristic, suspicion. Their fate was

6

sealed in 1646 when word leaked out about a clandestine visit made by the defeated King Charles and Little Gidding was ransacked by way of a reprisal. Despite this, the Community survived for at least another decade, but the manor house slowly became a family home again.

The present community, established in the 1970s, attempts to follow the moderate, practical, domestic, lay, optimistic pattern adopted by Nicholas Ferrar. Currently made up of some forty members of all ages and denominations, it is held together by a daily office, a weekly ecumenical communion, and lots of parties.

The Book

'Flavia will sometimes read a book of piety, if it is a short one, if it is much commended for style and language, and she can tell where to borrow it.'

William Law, *A Serious Call to a Devout and Holy Life*

A number of considerations lie behind the selection of pieces for this book. First of all we have made an attempt to portray the history of English spirituality. This has been built on a skeleton of what we consider the most prominent spiritual writers. When considering their work we have felt at liberty to select both the key passages and the less well-known ones, aiming all the time to provide some sort of representative sample of their writing and thought.

We have been keen to produce a useful book, which readers, if they so wish, can refer to in their devotions. The majority of the pieces assembled here have survived not because of their literary value but because they have been inspirational. They still are.

Nevertheless, we have had no qualms about including a large number of what might be thought of as 'writers of literature' rather than of spirituality – well-known secular writers rather than divines. These are not people who *should* have shaped the English spirit, they are people who *did*.

For this reason we are not very apologetic for the fact that we have spent little time sifting through volumes of nineteenth century sermons. We think we have uncovered enough lost gems in the less obscure works dealt with here.

We have kept fairly strictly to our geographical limits, despite the regret it has caused, but have succumbed to naturalised Englishmen like Von Hügel and T. S. Eliot. Of course English spirituality has not grown up isolated from the influence of other nations, but the Scottish, the Welsh, the Irish, the French, the Germans and so on all have their own brand of spirituality. We shall not poach their nationals, but leave them to their own anthologists.

We gave some thought to the inclusion of hymns, not least because the ones we chose are naturally the most familiar. Nevertheless, a good hymn (and many a bad one) has influenced far more people from a wider social spectrum than most of the other poetry or prose here. Moreover, we have been at liberty to select some hymns condemned to an undeserved obscurity on account of their (usually reluctant) marriage to atrocious tunes.

Ultimately, though, we have tried to find good, lively, interesting, helpful pieces, regardless of author or history or format. They are here not because we think they *ought* to be included, but because we have enjoyed them.

Our hope is that by providing a glimpse of the whole history and range of English spirituality, we might jog people's memories about ideas which have been forgotten, provide a corrective to some of the lopsided spirituality being taught today, and demonstrate to people the rich variety that has gone to form their own spiritual character.

Caedmon
d.680?

This hymn is the only surviving work attributable to Caedmon, and the story behind it is more remarkable than its content. According to Bede, Caedmon was an unschooled herdsman until, one night, a heavenly visitor commanded him to sing about the creation of the world. What follows is the result. Caedmon joined the abbey at Whitby and spent his remaining days composing songs and his name is the first known in English poetry.

Now must we praise the Guardian of heaven,
The power and conception of the Lord,
And all His works, as He, eternal Lord,
Father of glory, started every wonder.
First he created heaven as a roof,
The holy Maker, for the sons of men.
Then the eternal Keeper of mankind
Furnished the earth below, the land for men,
Almighty God and everlasting Lord.

The Venerable Bede
673–735

Bede (he was first called 'Venerable' in the ninth century) spent most of his life as a monk at Jarrow. He wrote nearly forty works, a phenomenal output at that time, his most famous being his history of the English Church.

Almsgiving

Well shall it be for the just-minded man
Who has within himself a spacious heart;
That shall bring greatest honour in the world
And best of judgement for him from our Lord.
And just as he could quench the surging flame
With water, that it might no longer harm
The brightly burning city, even so
Does he by almsgiving cast right away
The wounds of sinfulness, and heal his soul.

9

Bede's Death Song

Before the journey that awaits us all,
No man becomes so wise that he has not
Need to think out, before his going hence
What judgement will be given to his soul
After his death, of evil or of good.

[One of King Edwin's chief men gives his advice on whether they should accept the faith of Christ, A.D. 627:]

'Your Majesty, when we compare the present life of man with that time of which we have no knowledge, it seems to me like the swift flight of a lone sparrow through the banqueting-hall where you sit in the winter months to dine with your thanes and counsellors. Inside there is a comforting fire to warm the room; outside, the wintry storms of snow and rain are raging. This sparrow flies swiftly in through one door of the hall, and out through another. While he is inside, he is safe from the winter storms; but after a few moments of comfort, he vanishes from sight into the darkness whence he came. Similarly, man appears on earth for a little while, but we know nothing of what went before this life, and what follows. Therefore if this new teaching can reveal any more certain knowledge, it seems only right that we should follow it.'

A History of the English Church and People

St Cuthbert
d.687

This is one of the saints' lives which were an important source of inspiration for the Church from its earliest days. Cuthbert was abbot and later bishop of Lindisfarne and made long solitary journeys to minister to remote villages.

St Cuthbert in the Sheiling

One day as he rode his solitary way about the third hour after sunrise, he came by chance upon a hamlet a spear's cast

10

from the track, and turned off the road to it. The woman of the house that he went into was the pious mother of a family and he was anxious to rest there a little while and to ask some provision for the horse that carried him rather than for himself, for it was the oncoming of winter. The woman brought him kindly in, and was earnest with him that he would let her get ready a meal, for his own comfort, but the man of God denied her. 'I must not eat yet,' said he, 'because today is a fast.' It was indeed Friday when the faithful for the most part prolong their fast until the third hour before sunset, for reverence of the Lord's Passion. The woman, full of hospitable zeal, insisted. 'See now,' said she, 'the road that you are going, you will never find a clachan or a single house upon it, and indeed you have a long way yet before you, and you will not be at the end of it before sundown. So do, I ask you, take some food before you go, or you will have to keep your fast the whole day, and maybe even till the morrow.' But though she pressed him hard, devotion to his religion overcame her entreating, and he went through the day fasting, until evening.

But as twilight fell and he began to see that he could not come to the end of the journey he had planned that day, and that there was no human habitation near where he could stay the night, suddenly as he rode he saw close by a huddle of shepherds' huts, built ramshackle for the summer, and now lying open and deserted. Thither he went in search of shelter, tethered his horse to the inside wall, gathered up a bundle of hay that the wind had torn from the thatch, and set it before him for fodder. Himself had begun to say his hours, when suddenly in the midst of his chanting of the Psalms he saw his horse rear up his head and begin cropping the thatch of the hovel and dragging it down, and in the middle of the falling thatch came tumbling a linen cloth lapped up: curious to know what it might be, he finished his prayer, came up and found wrapped in the linen cloth a piece of loaf still hot, and meat, enough for one man's meal. And chanting his thanks for heaven's grace, 'I thank God,' said he, 'Who has stooped to make a feast for me that was fasting for love of His Passion, and for my comrade.' So he divided the piece of loaf that he had found, and gave half to the horse, and the rest he kept for himself to eat, and from that day he was the readier to fasting because he understood that the meal had been prepared for him in the solitude by His gift Who of old fed Elijah the solitary in like fashion by the birds, when there was no man near to minister to him, Whose eyes are on them that fear Him and that hope in His mercy, that He will snatch their souls from death and cherish them in their hunger. And this story I had from a brother of our monastery which is at the mouth of the river Wear, a priest, Ingwald by name, who has the grace of his great age rather to contemplate things eternal with a pure heart than things temporal with the eyes of earth: and he said that he had it from Cuthbert himself, the time that he was bishop.

– a story told by Bede

Riddle
8th century

An example of the sophisticated wit of the so-called 'Dark Ages'. The Saxons, who developed the riddle form first in Latin then in the vernacular, were indiscriminating about their subject matter, religious riddles rubbing shoulders with obscene ones.

Some enemy deprived me of my life
And took away my worldly strength, then wet me,
Dipped me in water, took me out again,
Set me in sunshine, where I quickly lost
The hairs I had. Later the knife's hard edge
Cut me with all impurities ground off.
Then fingers folded me; the bird's fine raiment
Traced often over me with useful drops
Across my brown domain, swallowed the tree-dye
Mixed up with water, stepped on me again
Leaving dark tracks. The hero clothed me then
With boards to guard me, stretched hide over me,
Decked me with gold; and thus the splendid work
Of smiths, with wire bound round, embellished me.
Now my red dye and all my decorations,

My gorgeous trappings far and wide proclaim
The Lord of Hosts, not grief for foolish sins.
If sons of men will make good use of me,
By that they shall be sounder, more victorious,
Their hearts more bold, their minds more full of joy,
Their spirits wiser; they shall have more friends,
Dear ones and kinsmen, truer and more good,
More kind and faithful, who will add more glory
And happiness by favours, who will lay
Upon them kindnesses and benefits,
And clasp them fast in the embrace of love.
Say who I am, useful to men. My name
Is famous, good to men, and also sacred.

[The Bible]

The Dream of the Rood
8th century

A strange and beautiful poem written from an unusual angle – from the point of view of the rood (or cross) on which Christ was crucified. The image of the suffering, human Christ was still five centuries off; the victim here is a kingly warrior.

Hear while I tell about the best of dreams
Which came to me the middle of one night
While humankind were sleeping in their beds.
It was as though I saw a wondrous tree
Towering in the sky suffused with light . . .
                                    . . . the best
Of woods began to speak these words to me:
'It was long past – I still remember it –
That I was cut down at the copse's end,
Moved from my roots. Strong enemies there took me,
Told me to hold aloft their criminals,
Made me a spectacle. Men carried me
Upon their shoulders, set me on a hill,
A host of enemies there fastened me.
And then I saw the Lord of all mankind

13

Hasten with eager zeal that He might mount
Upon me. I durst not against God's word
Bend down or break, when I saw tremble all
The surface of the earth. Although I might
Have struck down all the foes, yet stood I fast.
Then the young hero (who was God almighty)
Got ready, resolute and strong in heart.
He climbed onto the lofty gallows-tree,
Bold in the sight of many watching men,
When he intended to redeem mankind.
I trembled as the warrior embraced me.
But still I dared not bend down to the earth,
Fall to the ground. Upright I had to stand.
A rood I was raised up; and I held high
The noble King, the Lord of heaven above.
I dared not stoop. They pierced me with dark nails;
The scars can still be clearly seen on me,
The open wounds of malice. Yet might I
Not harm them. They reviled us both together.
I was made wet all over with the blood
Which poured out from His side, after He had
Sent forth His spirit. And I underwent
Full many a dire experience on that hill.
I saw the God of hosts stretched grimly out.
Darkness covered the Ruler's corpse with clouds,
His shining beauty; the shadows passed across,
Black in the darkness. All creation wept,
Bewailed the King's death; Christ was on the cross.
And yet I saw men coming from afar,
Hastening to the Prince. I watched it all.'

St Edmund (King)
841–869

*The influence of saints' lives stretches into this century, some of them
passed on through the oral tradition. This account of the martyrdom of
King Edmund was told to writer Julian Tennyson in the 1930s by a
man of Hoxne, Suffolk, the site of the execution. Edmund showed
kindness to the king of the Danes who was then murdered by Edmund's
chief manservant. The Danes set out to avenge their king and, when
the English army had been defeated, the fugitive Edmund was betrayed
to the invaders by a young courting couple as he hid under Hoxne
bridge . . .*

. . . Oh ah, that surely was a rotten trick, this ere cupple they
went off an fitched the Deens, ould Luddy's two sons an the
whull blessed army, they come a runnin up an took ahowd
o' young Edmund an hulled im out from under the little ould
bridge. 'Oho, me little king-o,' they say, 'yew're ketched now
an yew're a goin to be kilt an no mistake. But ere's one thing,'
they say, 'will yew give up yer Chrisheranity afore yew're
kilt, y'know kind o' change yer relijun like, cause thass the
wrong un yew got there, boy.' But young Edmund he was a
werry kerajus chap, he whully stuck by what he thot was
roight, dew they moight ha let im orf. 'I ain't a goin to give
up nuthen fer yew,' he say, 'yew're a rotten lot o' barstids
the whull bloody bag of ye.' 'Thass all roight, boy,' they say,
'we on't waste na more time then,' they hulled im orf to a
fild an tied im to a owk tree an they took the whip to im, like
a lot o' savidges they was, han't no marcy fer the pore boy.
Howsever, they din't kill im that way, they shot all their
arrers into im an they then cut is hid orf, an thass how they
left im under that ould tree an then went orf arter a lot more
davilry all ower the country . . .

Well, thass pretty near the ind about little ould Edmund.
Arter he was did is frinds come 'long an fount is copse a layin
there, the Deens ad trew is hid away time they cut that orf,
an they say, 'Look ere,' they say, 'we carn't bury this ere
without we find the hid fust.' So they set about an look fer
that, they went into a wood 'longside an by'nby they started

15

a cullin out to axe the hid where that'd got tew. Thass a marvellous funny thing, suthen went an shruck out 'Hare, hare, hare,' an that was th'ould hid, thass allus fared to me like a bit o' friction [fiction] I must say. Howsever, they come up an fount a bloomin gret oolf [wolf] got ahowd o' that in is pors, an he runned orf, an what d'yew think? That there ould oolf he kep a runnin about the filds wi' that hid an that was a two-tree weeks afore he gin that up. Thass a rum un, ain't it, how he din't want to let that goo? Howsever, he set down one day an he kep that in is pors till they come up with im, an dret if he din't then give that up as jintle as a dawg with a bard.

They took that hid an so sune as they set that down that went an jined up wi the buddy, roight afore their bloomin eyes, time they stood a gawpin like a lot of ould fish. 'Well, thass rum doins, that is,' they say, 'there's ony one meanin to that. This ere Edmund he's a blessed saint.'

Recorded in *Suffolk Scene*

St Anselm
1033–1109

Anselm was abbot in the Norman Abbey of Bec, and then became Archbishop of Canterbury. He was frequently involved in political and religious conflict, and was twice exiled by the King. He is best known as a theologian and philosopher, but also composed a new kind of poetry, for use in silent and private meditation.

Come now, little child.
Turn awhile from your daily work;
hide yourself for a little time from your restless thoughts,
cast away your troublesome cares;
put aside your wearisome distractions.
Give yourself a little leisure to talk with God,
and rest awhile in him.
Enter the secret chamber of your heart,
shutting out everything but God,
and that which may help you in seeking him.

And when you've closed the door, seek him.
Now, my whole heart, say to God:
'I seek your face;
your face, O Lord, do I seek.'

I will seek you by desiring you,
and desire you in seeking you.
I will find you by loving you,
and love you in finding you.
I praise and give thanks to you
that you have made me in your image,
so that I can remember you,
think of you,
love you.
But so darkened is your image in me
by the smoke of my sins,
that it is useless unless you restore it.
I do not seek, O Lord, to search out your depths,
but only in some measure to understand your truth,
which my heart believes and loves.
I do not seek to understand so that I may believe,
but believe that I may understand.
For this I know to be true:
that unless I first believe I shall not understand.

The Proslogian

A Meditation on the Miseries of this Life

Imagine a deep and dark valley, full of all manner of torments, and spanned only by a long, narrow bridge, the width of a man's foot. A traveller is compelled to pass over this straight, high, perilous bridge; his eyes are blindfolded so that he cannot see his steps; his hands are bound behind him so that he cannot guide himself by using a stick. How great is the fear and distress of that man! Do you think he can find a place in his thoughts for cheerfulness, merriment or wantonness? I think not. Pride and vainglory have deserted him; only the darkness of death remains in his mind. Imagine, moreover, a multitude of savage birds hovering around the bridge, seeking to drag the traveller down into the abyss. Will not his fears be multiplied? And what if each plank is withdrawn

17

as soon as he has passed over it? Is not his dread the more greatly increased?

Now, consider the significance of this image and allow a godly fear and trembling to take hold of your mind. The deep and dark valley represents hell, which is an immeasurable abyss, made terrible by the shadows of black darkness, and the multitude of torments. There is nothing in the abyss to soothe, but only those things that cause appalling distress. The perilous bridge is this present life, and the planks that are withdrawn are the days of our life, which pass away never to return, but by growing fewer press us on towards our goal. The birds that hover around the bridge are the evil spirits which endlessly seek to hurl travellers down into the abyss. We ourselves are the travellers that pass over, blindfolded by our ignorance and bound by the chain of the difficulty of doing good works, so that we cannot direct our steps freely towards God in holiness of life.

Consider, therefore, whether you should not cry out to your Creator, so that, defended by his protection, you may sing in faith among the multitude of your enemies: 'The Lord is my light and my salvation; whom shall I fear?' He is your light against blindness; your salvation against difficulty.

Meditation

Grant, Lord, that we may hold to you without parting,
Worship you without wearying,
Serve you without failing;
Faithfully seek you,
Happily find you,
And for ever possess you,
The only God,
Blessed, now and for ever.

Let me seek you in my desire,
Let me desire you in my seeking.
Let me find you by loving you,
Let me love you when I find you.

Prayers

18

St Godric
c.1065–1170

*Reputed to have been a pirate in the earlier part of his long life, Godric
spent his last sixty years in a hut by the River Wear near Durham.
Like a traditional saint he is said to have had an affinity with animals
and kept poisonous snakes as pets until he found they distracted his
prayers.*

St Godric at Finchale

I myself as a small boy saw the great Godric, I a youngster
and he an old man, and the high memory of it is sweet in
my mind. He was small enough in body, but his spirit had
the height of heaven. In youth indeed his hair was black, but
in his old age, of an angelic whiteness: a broad forehead,
sparkling eyes, heavy eyebrows that almost met, broad shoulders, a lean body, thin with fasting . . . He was a monk of
Durham, and for sixty years lived a hermit: he died an old
man and full of days in his chosen dwelling place in Finchale:
and being dead, his virtue speaketh . . .

At his first coming [to Finchale] he had built an oratory and
one day saw above the altar two young and very lovely maids:
the one of them, Mary Magdalene, the other the Mother of
God: and the Mother of God put her hand upon his head
and taught him to sing after her this prayer:

[See next piece]

Thereafter with more devotion than ever he served the Lord:
and called upon the most blessed Mother of God, even as he
had promised her, in all distress that came about him, and
found her most swift to aid.

> – from lives of St Godric by Geoffrey and Reginald of
> Durham

Sainte Marye Virgine,
Moder Jesu Christes Nazarene,
Onfo, schild, help thin Godric,
Onfang, bring heyilich with thee in Godes Riche.

Sainte Marye, Christes bur,
Maidenes clenhad, modered flur,
Dilie min sinne, rix in min mod,
Bring me to winne with the self God.

*[St Mary the Virgin, Mother of Jesus Christ of Nazareth, receive,
shield and help your Godric, (and) having received (him), bring
(him) on high with you into God's Kingdom.*

*St Mary, Christ's bower, virgin among maidens, flower of motherhood,
blot out my sin, reign in my heart, bring me to prosperity with that
same God.]*

St Aelred of Rievaulx
1110–1163

*Aelred was descended from two generations of Saxon priests in Hexham
and became abbot of the 600-strong Cistercian monastery at Rievaulx
in Yorkshire. His rule was marked by his gentleness and friendliness.
He was a major influence in the 'humanising' of Christ which took
place in the early Middle Ages.*

The Creator and His Creatures

But what is this love which I desire, O my God? Unless I
am much misled, it is a wonderful delight in the soul, which
is the more sweet for being unsullied by passion, more sincere
if it is tender, and a source of joy when it embraces all our
fellow men. Love may truly be called the heart's own sense
of taste, since it enables us to feel Thy sweetness. Love is the
eye by means of which we can see that Thou art good. Love
is a capacity for God who transcends all things, and whoever
loves God gathers God to himself.

The Will as Love

Our love of God must not be gauged by the passing feelings
we experience that are not controlled by the will, but rather
we must judge them by the enduring quality of the will itself.
For loving God means that we join our will to God's will. It

means that our will consents to whatever the will of God commands. It means that we have only one reason for wishing anything, and the reason is that we know that God wills it . . .

The visitations of God's grace that come to us in the form of feelings and emotions, are for God to bestow when and where and to whom He wills. It is not for us to seek them, or even to ask for them, and if God should suddenly remove them from us, our wills must be in agreement with His. For the man who loves God is the man who bears patiently with all that God does to him, and who is zealous in carrying out God's precepts.

A Distinction between Two Loves

Feelings are not entirely ours to command. We are attracted towards some against our will, while towards others we can never experience a spontaneous affection. If we are moved solely by our feelings, that is not love. Real love means that we are still master of our acts, and we use our inclinations and attractions simply as guides in the direction which we choose to take. And the same is true when reason tells us what direction love must take. It is not reason which impels us to love, it is we ourselves who choose to love, taking reason as our guide.

Reasonable Inclinations

Reasonable inclinations are those which arise from the contemplation of another's virtues; these are the best means we have for increasing our love towards our fellow men. The love of virtue in others is indeed a good indication that we have some little virtue in ourselves.

The Love of Kindred

A friend cannot but be loved. Therefore we must take care to love him in God. But someone towards whom we can feel no attraction, whom we cannot love for his own sake, is loved for God's sake alone. When we love our friends, we do so according to our inclination. But towards those to whom we are not attracted as friends, reason is our guide.

21

The Enjoyment of Friendship

The sweetness of God that we taste in this life is given us, not so much for enjoyment as for a consolation and encouragement for our weakness. That is why it is such a great joy to have the consolation of someone's affection – someone to whom one is deeply united by the bonds of love; someone in whom our weary spirit may find rest, and to whom we may pour out our souls . . . someone whose conversation is as sweet as a song in the tedium of our daily life. He must be someone whose soul will be to us a refuge to creep into when the world is altogether too much for us; someone to whom we can confide all our thoughts. His spirit will give us the comforting kiss that heals all the sickness of our preoccupied hearts. He will weep with us when we are troubled, and rejoice with us when we are happy, and he will always be there to consult when we are in doubt. And we will be so deeply bound to him in our hearts that even when he is far away, we shall find him together with us in spirit, together and alone.

Enjoying in the Lord

If we love our friends for the consolation of their company, let our conversation be about good and serious things; let us reflect on the problems of life, and the guidance we get from the scriptures in these matters. We can share the burdens of our daily lives, and the hope of our future happiness that makes us happy even now as we look forward to it together. We can share our secret thoughts and strive together in our longing for the sight of Jesus' face. And when we do take a rest from more serious pursuits (as indeed we must occasionally) even though our pastimes may not be particularly elevating, at least let there be nothing bad about them, nothing foolish. We must enjoy one another . . . and our enjoyment must be in justice, so that we may exhort one another in a spirit of freedom. We need to correct one another at times, and must not forget that even if a friend's corrections make us smart, they are worth far more to us than all the false endearments of those who do not love us at all.

The Mirror of Charity

22

St Edmund of Abingdon
1175–1240

The son of a wealthy Oxford merchant, Edmund was made Archbishop in 1233, and in his first week in office threatened King Henry III with excommunication if he did not improve his government. Despite the political turmoil of the next seven years, his personal saintliness and purity of motive were much admired, except perhaps by Henry, who opposed his canonisation in 1247.

What It Is to Live Perfectly

To live perfectly is to live honourably, meekly and charitably, and to live honourably is to set your intention on doing God's will. Before doing any thing, consider if it is God's will: whether it is thinking in your heart, or saying with your mouth; indeed, even if it is seeing with your eyes, hearing with your ears, smelling with your nose, tasting with your tongue, touching with your hands; walking or standing, lying or sitting. If it is God's will, then do it with all your might; and if it is not His will, then suffer death rather than attempt it.

If you ask me 'What is God's will?' I will answer that His will is that you become holy.

What Makes Man Holy

If you ask me 'What makes a man holy?' I will tell you that it is knowledge and love: the knowledge of truth and the love of goodness. You can only come to the knowledge of God and His truth, by knowing yourself; and you can only come to the love of God by loving your fellow Christians.

By diligent meditation you will come to know yourself; and by pure contemplation you will come to know God.

Of Contemplation

In the first degree of contemplation the soul is led into itself and gathered within itself. In the second degree man sees what he is, so gathered together. In the third degree man lifts himself above himself, and takes pains to look on his God in

23

his own nature. He can only come to himself in this way when he has learnt to tread down every imagination that comes to his heart, and to refrain from every distraction that assails his bodily senses. Only then may he see himself as he is, without a body . . .

Think how great your soul is: you can comprehend heaven and earth, and all that is in them, with only a thought. Yet your soul is too great and noble for any creature to understand it perfectly. How great and noble is God, who made noble things out of nothing! He is above all things, and within all things, without all things and beneath all things. He is above all things, governing them; beneath all things, bearing them; within all things, fulfilling them; without all things, surrounding them.

To contemplate in this way encourages steadfast faith and solid devotion. Afterwards you will think how generous God is in so many ways. He is generous with earthly goods, giving good things to evil people as well as to those who are good. He is generous in His forgiveness; for however much wrong a man does to God, He is a hundred times more ready to forgive than that wretched soul would be to ask forgiveness.

The Mirror of St Edmund

Ancrene Riwle
c.1220

The 'Anchoresses' Rule' – also known as the Ancrene Wisse – *is addressed to three sisters living in Herefordshire who had given up everything (except their maid-servants) to live as recluses. The author, thought by one scholar to be Brian of Lingen, a secular brother at Wigmore Abbey, sets them a rigorous rule of prayer combined with spiritual advice and encouragement.*

Nothing subdues wild flesh nor tames it more than much watching, for watchfulness is praised in many places in Holy Scripture. 'Therefore, if you do not want to fall into temptations,' says our Lord, 'watch and pray.'

Eight things in particular persuade and invite us to be

watchful and about some good work: the shortness of this life; the difficulty of our way; our merits which are so few; our sins which are so many; knowing we are sure to die but not knowing when; the severe judgement of doomsday; the torments of hell – of which consider three things – the innumerable pain which no tongue may tell, the eternity of each of these and their great bitterness. The eighth thing is the greatness of the reward in the bliss of heaven, world without end.

The swine of greediness, called gluttony, has piglets with these names: the first is called Too Early; the second, Too Daintily; the third, Too Voraciously; the fourth, Too Much; the fifth, Too Often, in drink more than in meat. In this way these pigs are farrowed. I only mention them briefly, my dear sisters, for I am not afraid that you feed them.

Bodily temptation may be compared to a foot wound; spiritual temptation, which should be dreaded more, may, because of the danger, be called a breast wound. But it seems to us that bodily temptations are the greater, because we feel them more. The other we do not notice, though we have them often, yet they are horrendous to God's bright eyes.

They are, therefore, to be dreaded much more. Men look to doctors and medicine for a flesh wound, which they feel instantly. But spiritual hurts do not feel sore and so they are not healed with confession nor with penitence. They draw men on to eternal death before they are in the least aware of them.

Every worldly affliction is God's ambassador. Men will gladly honour and welcome the messenger from a man of rank, and so much the more if he is an intimate of the King of Heaven. And who was closer to the King while he lived on earth than this ambassador, that is, worldly suffering, who never left him till the end of his life? God loved me and sent me to his friend, says this messenger. My coming and my abiding, though it seems bitter, is yet salutary.

There was a lady who was besieged by her foes within an

earthen castle, and her land all destroyed, and herself quite poor. The love of a powerful king was, however, fixed upon her with such boundless affection, that to solicit her love he sent his ambassadors, one after another, and often many together, and sent her jewels both many and fair, and supplies of victuals, and the aid of his noble army to keep her castle. She received them all as a careless creature, that was so hard-hearted that he could never get any nearer to her love.

What more would you have? He came himself at last and showed her his fair face, as one who was of all men the most beautiful to behold; and spoke most sweetly, and such pleasant words, that they might have raised the dead from death to life. And he performed many miracles, and did many wondrous works before her eyes, and showed her his power, told her of his kingdom, and offered to make her queen of all that belonged to him.

All this availed nothing. Was not this disdain a marvellous thing? For she was never worthy to be his kitchen maid. But, through his goodness and gentleness, love so overmastered him that he at last said, 'Lady, thou art attacked, and thy enemies are so strong that, without help of me, thou canst not by any means escape their hands, so that they may not put thee to a shameful death, I will, for the love of thee, take upon me this fight, and deliver thee from those who seek thy death.

'Yet I know assuredly that among them I shall receive a mortal wound, and I will gladly receive it to win thy heart. Now then, I beseech thee, for the love that I show thee, that thou love me, at least after being thus done to death, since thou would not in my lifetime.'

This the king did so in every point. He delivered her from all her enemies, and was himself grievously maltreated, and at last slain. But by a miracle, he arose from death to life.

Would not this lady be of a most perverse nature, if she did not love him, after this, above all things?

Next to your flesh you should not wear flaxen cloth, unless it is made of hards and of coarse canvas. Whoever wishes to wear a stamin [a rough shirt] may; those who do not, need not. You shall sleep in a garment and a girt. Wear no iron, nor haircloth, nor hedgehog skins; and do not beat yourselves with these, nor with scourges of leather or leaded thongs; and do not make yourselves bleed with briars without permission from your confessor; and do not, at any one time, use too many flagellations. Let your shoes be thick and warm.

Richard Rolle
c.1300–1349

At the age of 19 Rolle abandoned his studies in Oxford and returned to his home in north Yorkshire to be a hermit. 'My brother is mad!' exclaimed his sister when he borrowed two of her dresses in order to look the part. His burning love of Christ stayed with him, however, and he became widely respected as a preacher and confessor.

Prologue

I was more astonished than I showed the first time I felt my heart burn with fire. The sensation was not imaginary: I felt real warmth. I was amazed at the way the fire burst up in my soul and gave me unexpected comfort, and I kept touching my breast to see if there was some physical cause. Once I knew that the fire had been spiritually kindled within me and was nothing to do with earthly love or material cause, then I was assured that it was the gift of my Maker. And so I am glad to melt into a desire of greater love; and especially I rejoice at the wonderful delight and spiritual sweetness of this holy flame which so comforts my mind.

Before this moment I had no idea that we exiles could know such comfortable and sweet devotion: for truly my heart was as inflamed as if a real fire were burning there.

Why it is better to prefer the love of God to intellectual argument

Let us seek the love of Christ burning within us, rather than involve ourselves in unprofitable disputes, for when we argue and discuss amongst ourselves we cannot feel the sweetness of eternity. So many people nowadays seek knowledge rather than love; they seem hardly to know what love is or to feel its delights. Yet really all their work and discourse should lead them to the fire of God's love. They should be ashamed of themselves. An old woman can know more of God's love, and less of worldly pleasures, than the brilliant theologian whose study is in vain.

That God's love is for every time and occasion, and never fails

If we are true lovers of our Lord Jesus Christ, we can think of him when we are travelling, and have a song of love in our hearts when we are in company. He can be our companion at mealtimes, even as we eat and drink . . . and while we work we can lift our hearts to heaven and retain our knowledge of eternal love. At every moment we can know that Christ is close to us, and nothing but sleep need take him from our thoughts.

The love of God is to be found in fervour, song and sweetness

I call it 'fervour' when the heart and the mind are ablaze with eternal love. One can feel a fire burning within.

I call it 'song' when there is in the heart a spirit of everlasting praise. The soul sings in perfect harmony with heaven, and the mind is enchanted by the song.

Fervour and song arise from the utmost devotion, and together they bring an indescribable sweetness . . . These sensations are not mere illusions, but are the most exquisite result of all our deeds.

Let songs of love be our comfort and sweet devotion our delight

O honey-sweet heat, sweeter than all delight, more delectable than all riches.
My God! My Love! come into me; thrill me with your love; wound me with your beauty.
Smother me with your comfort; give your healing balm to your feeble lover, and show yourself to me.
For you are all that I desire, all that I seek.
My heart yearns for you, and my body thirsts for you.
But you do not come to me: you turn your face away.

28

You bolt the door and hide yourself; and laugh at my sufferings.

Yet even so, you seize your lovers and carry them away from earthly things, lifting them above their worldly desires. You take them and show them how to love you and how to live in love. And so they sing their praises to you in spiritual songs that burn within and overflow; and in this sweetness they feel the dart of love.

O lovely Eternal Love, that raised us from the depths and showed us the wonder of your divine Majesty. Come to me, my Love! I gave up all I had for you. I shunned all that might have been mine, so that my soul might be a home and source of comfort for you. Do not forsake me when you know I am glowing with desire for you; when you know that my most burning desire is to be embraced by you. Give me grace to love you and to rest in you, that in your kingdom I may be worthy of seeing you without end.

I know of no sweeter delight than to sing to you and praise you in my heart, Jesus my love. I know of no greater or more plenteous joy than to feel the sweet heat of love in my mind . . .

Come, my Saviour, and comfort my soul; make me constant in my love, that I may never cease to love you.

The Fire of Love

Whanne Ic Se on Rode
early 14th century

By the fourteenth century, Western Christians were concentrating on the Passion and the sufferings of Christ. In this typical lyric, the stark image of Christ on the cross is contrasted with a language of great intimacy and endearment – 'my lemman' = 'my lover'.

Whanne ic[1] se on Rode
Jesu, my lemman,
And besiden him stonden
Marye and Johan,
And his rig[2] iswongen,[3]
And his side istungen,
For the luve of man;
Well ou[4] ic to wepen,
And sinnes for to leten,[5]
Yif ic of luve can,[6]
Yif ic of luve can,
Yif ic of luve can.

1 I   2 back   3 scourged   4 ought   5 leave   6 know

The Cloud of Unknowing
c.1370

The Cloud is the most well-known English mystical work, but nothing is known of its author except that he probably came from the north-east Midlands. He is writing for a mature contemplative and argues that the concerns of this world must be lost in a cloud of forgetting before one can pierce God's dwelling, the cloud of unknowing.

Spiritual friend in God, according to my rough and ready reflections, there are four degrees or kinds of Christian life: ordinary, special, solitary and perfect. The first three may begin and end in this life, and by grace the fourth may also be begun here, but it goes on without end in the bliss of heaven. You will notice I have written them in a sequence (ordinary, special, solitary, perfect); and I think it is this very order and by the desire of your heart, that our Lord, in his abundant mercy, has called you and led you to himself . . .

He has kindled your desire, and in his gracious way he has bound you by a chain of deep longing and led you to a more special state of life, where you have learnt to live more spiritually in his service than you could have done in the ordinary way.

And there is more: he is not content to leave you there. Because of the deep love he has for you, he has called you to the third state of life: the solitary. Through the life of the solitary you will learn how to reach out to the way of life which is perfect, the last state of all . . .

So I beg you, press on with all speed. Look ahead, not behind; look for what you need, not what you already have; and then you will find humility. Your life must become a life of longing if you are to achieve perfection, and this longing must stem from the depth of your desires . . . Guard your spiritual windows and doors against the attacks of the enemy, and seek God humbly in prayer; he will help you. Call upon him, for he is most willing and only waiting for you.

You ask me, 'What am I to do? How can I move him?'

Lift up your heart to God in humble and total love, and aim only at God, not his blessings nor his rewards. Indeed, refuse to think of anything but God himself.

At first you will find only darkness, a cloud of unknowing as it were; you cannot tell what it is, except that you feel a simple intent to reach out to God. This darkness, this cloud, remains between you and your God whatever you do, and prevents you from seeing him in the clear light of understanding, or from experiencing him in the sweet love of affection. Accept, therefore, that you must wait in darkness for as long as is needful, and continue to long for him whom you love. For if ever you are to see him or experience him in this life, it will be in this cloud and this darkness. If you work diligently at what I tell you, I trust, by his mercy, you will come to your heart's desire . . .

Do not make the mistake of thinking that the cloud I speak of is like the clouds of the sky, or that the darkness is like the darkness of your room at night when the candle is blown out. Such clouds and darkness can be produced in

31

your mind's eye even on the brightest day of summer, just as you can imagine a clear shining light on the darkest night of winter. No, I mean nothing of this sort. By 'darkness' I mean a lack of knowing, just as the things you have never known or have forgotten are dark to you, for you cannot see them in your imagination. It is not a cloud of the sky, but a cloud of unknowing that is between you and your God . . .

But now you ask me, 'How am I to think of God himself, and what is he?' and I can only reply, 'I have no idea!' For your question brings me to the same darkness, to the same cloud of unknowing, that I wish you to be brought to! Although by grace we can come to understand the workings of most things, including the workings of God, yet we cannot know God himself. Therefore, I wish to leave aside all that I can think of, and choose instead to love the very thing I cannot conceive. For even though God cannot be comprehended, he can be loved. By love, not thought, he can be taken and held.

So although it is good sometimes to think of God's kindness and worthiness – indeed it is a part of contemplation – yet for the work in hand it must be pushed aside and covered with a cloud of forgetting. Step lovingly away from it, and firmly and devoutly pierce the darkness above you with impulsive love. Strive to pierce that thick cloud of unknowing with a sharp dart of longing love; and, come what may, do not give up.

Humility is mysteriously and perfectly contained in this blind, impulsive love, as it beats upon the dark cloud of unknowing, and strives to put down and forget all other things. And the same is true of all the virtues, especially charity. For charity means nothing else but the love of God for himself above all other things, and the love of other people, for God's sake, equal to the love of yourself. It is clear that in this work God is loved for himself above all creatures. For the essence of what you are doing is nothing but a simple and direct reaching out to God alone.

It is not what you are or what you have been that God looks at with his merciful eyes, but what you desire to be.

The Cloud of Unknowing

'Pearl'
c.1375

The anonymous poet who wrote the four poems, Pearl, Sir Gawain and the Green Knight, Patience *and* Cleanness *is believed to have come from the north-west Midlands. In* Pearl, *thought by some to have an autobiographical root, a 'jeweller' dreams he meets his daughter, his 'pearl' who died at age of two. She describes her life as a queen in heaven, patiently answers his objections, and allows him a glimpse of the heavenly city . . .*

'Now I am here in your presence [says the jeweller] I implore you to forget our dispute and tell me instead what sort of life you lead. For I am glad to see that your condition has become one of honour and happiness – of all my joys that is the highest, the foundation of all my bliss.'

'Well, may that bliss remain with you,' replied the lady, beautiful in face and form, 'and you are welcome to stay here and walk with me, for now your speech is dear to me. I warn you that arrogance and pride are bitterly hated here. My Lord does not want to chide, and all who dwell near him are meek; so when you appear in his land you must be deeply devout, holy and meek. My Lord the Lamb loves all such behaviour; that is the foundation of all my bliss.

'A blissful life you say I lead, and you want to know my state in it. Well you know that when "your pearl" fell away, I was of a young and tender age. But my Lord the Lamb, through his divine power, took me as his bride, crowned me queen to live in happiness for all the days that will ever come. As his beloved, I am completely his and am made possessor of all his inheritance: his worth, his excellence and his noble lineage are at the root of all my bliss.'

'My dear,' said I, 'are you sure this is true? Do not be displeased if I speak in error, but are you really the queen of heaven, whom all this world should honour? We believe in Mary, source of grace, who bore a child though she was a virgin flower. Who could take the crown away from her unless they surpassed her in some grace? And yet her sweetness is

33

unique, because of which we call her the Phoenix of Arraby –
who flew flawless from her Creator; such is the Queen of
Courtesy.'

'O courteous Queen,' said the fair one, kneeling on the
ground and turning her face upwards, 'Peerless Mother and
fairest Maiden, blessed source of every grace!' She arose,
paused, then said to me: 'Sir, many contest here and win the
prize – but none are usurpers. That empress holds all
heaven – and earth and hell – in her power. No one could
chase her out of her inheritance, for she is the Queen of
Courtesy.

'The court in the kingdom of the living God has a property
all of its own: everyone who arrives there becomes either king
or queen of the whole realm. No one ever detracts from the
others but is instead gladdened by what they have. If it were
possible to change anything, they only wish that each crown
were worth five. But the Lady from whom Jesus sprung has
dominion over us all, and that displeases none of our
company, for she is the Queen of Courtesy.

'Out of courtesy, says Saint Paul, we are all members of
the body of Christ. Just as head and arm and leg and navel
are soundly joined to his body, so every Christian soul is a
limb belonging to him, the Master of Mysteries. Imagine if
any hatred or rancour existed between your own limbs; but
your head suffers neither anger nor resentment from your arm
or the finger on which you wear a ring. And so we behave
with love and joy towards the King and Queen of Courtesy.

'I accept that courtesy and great charity exist between
you,' I said, 'and forgive me if my speech offends you, but I
think you must have it completely wrong. What greater
reward, then, exists for someone who has remained steadfast
in this world, in life-long penitence, buying himself bliss with
bodily torment? What greater honour could he receive than
to be crowned King of Courtesy?

'That courtesy is handed out too freely, if what you say
is true. You lived not two years in our world; you never knew
how to please God nor how to pray; you didn't know the
"Our Father" or the Creed . . . and yet made queen on the
first day! I wasn't aware, so help me God, that God's world
followed such unjust ways. It might be proper, perhaps, for

you to hold the title of countess, or indeed, a lady of lower rank. But a queen! That is too high a state.'

'There is no limit to God's goodness,' that noble lady then replied, 'and all he ordains is good, for he can do nothing but what is right. As Matthew tells you in your mass book, in the truthful gospel of God almighty, he conceives a very apt example and compares it with the bright heavens . . .'

[The maiden here retells the parable of the workers who were hired late in the day to work in the vineyard and yet were still paid the same as the others.]

Then I spoke again and pointed out quite plainly: 'I think your tale is unreasonable. God is an alert judge and always supreme, or Holy Writ is just a fable. In the Psalter there is a verse, plain for all to see, which makes the point quite definitely: "You reward each one according to their deserts, O High King who pre-ordains everything." Now, if someone has remained faithful all his days and yet you get your payment before him, then it must mean that the less you work, the more you can take and so on: the less you do, the more you get.'

'There is no question of more and less in God's kingdom,' answered the maiden, 'for each person here is paid the same, whether they deserve little or much. For our noble Lord is no niggard, whether his dealings are gentle or hard. He pours out his gifts like water out of a ditch, or like mountain streams which never cease to flow. His mercy is abundant to those who shrink from sin and whom he rescues. For no bliss is withheld from them, so great is God's grace.

'But now by your arguments you are trying to shame me into thinking I was wrong to take my wages here. You say that because I came too late I am not worthy of so high a rank. But did you ever hear of any man who was so holy in his prayers that he did not at some time or in some way forfeit his right to a heavenly reward? And always the older they are, the more often they do wrong and forsake that right. Then mercy and grace must guide them to heaven – and thus great is the grace of God.

'But the innocent already have sufficient grace. As soon as they are born and make the customary descent into the waters of baptism: then they are brought into the vineyard. Quickly the light of day, into which darkness is creeping, sinks towards the night of death and the noble Lord pays wages to those who never did wrong before they left. They kept his commandments, they were in the vineyard; why should he not accept their labour, yes, and pay them first of all? For so great is God's grace.'

[Having spent some time persuading him further, the maiden grants his request for a glimpse of the New Jerusalem and leads him upstream to where he can see through the transparent crystal walls into the heart of the Holy City . . .]

Just as the mighty moon rises before the daylight has quite sunk down, so I suddenly became aware of a procession. Without any summons this noble city of rich renown was full of maidens all dressed in the same manner as my blessed one: all crowned in the same fashion, draped in pearls and wearing white; and bound firmly on each one's breast was the delightful pearl.

With great delight they glided in a company on golden streets which shone like glass. I am sure there were a hundred thousand, and all were alike in their appearance. It was hard to know who looked the most happy. The Lamb passed proudly before them with his seven horns of clear red gold; his clothing was as precious as pearls. Though they were many as they made their way towards the throne, there was no hurry in their company. Instead they moved forward with great delight, as meek as maidens seem at a mass.

It would be too much to tell of the delight at his coming, as the elders fell prostrate at his feet when he approached. Legions of angels summoned together scattered sweet-smelling incense. Then glory and happiness broke out anew, all singing songs of praise to that pretty jewel. As the angels sang of their joy, their voices must have pierced through the earth to hell. Indeed I myself took great delight in joining with his retinue to praise the Lamb.

My delight at gazing on the Lamb was so great that my mind became amazed. He was the best, the fairest, the most worthy of esteem that I ever heard tell of, his clothes glowing

white, his looks so meek and so noble. But I could see a
wound, wide and wet, close to his heart, his flesh cruelly torn.
Blood gushed out of his white side. Alas, thought I, who
could do this outrage? Any heart would have burned up
before he could have delighted in doing such a thing.

No one could have doubted the Lamb's delight, however.
Though he was wounded and hurt, it never showed in his
demeanour, so happy and glorious were his looks. I examined
his shining company and saw how they were brimming over
with everlasting life. And then I saw my little queen who had
stood beside me in the valley. Lord, how jolly she was among
her shining companions!

(lines 385–496; 601–636; 1093–1150)

Walter Hilton
d.1396

*Hilton grew up in the Midlands, and became a monk at an Augustinian
Priory at Thurgarton near Southwell. His mysticism was rooted in the
adoration of Christ on the cross, meditating both on the bitterness of
Christ's sufferings and the warmth of his compassion for humanity.
Hilton's writings contain much practical guidance for the aspiring
contemplative.*

**How a man who wishes to come to Jerusalem, the City
of Peace, which is contemplation, must have faith and
humility and endure troubles of body and soul:**

A true pilgrim going to Jerusalem leaves his house and land,
his wife and children, divesting himself of all that he possesses
in order to travel lightly. Likewise, if you will be a spiritual
pilgrim, you must rid yourself of all that you have, both good
deeds and bad, and throw them all behind you. In this way
there will be nothing of your own for you to lean on, and you
will desire more fully the grace of love and the spiritual
presence of Jesus. If you do this you will be set wholly and
fully on reaching Jerusalem, and no other place. That is to
say that your heart will be wholly and fully set on the love
of Jesus and the spiritual insights he is pleased to grant. For

that is the reason for your being: it is your purpose, your joy, your bliss. All else that you have and are is worthless without the inward confidence of this love. Take this to your heart, and cling to it, and it will keep you safe through the troubles and tumults of your pilgrimage.

How God opens the inner eye of the soul, not all at once, but gradually:

Three men are standing in the light of the sun. One of them is blind, the second can see but his eyes are closed, and the third has his eyes open. The blind man has no way of knowing that he is in the sun, apart from by believing the word of another. He represents a soul that is reformed through faith and believes the teaching of the church, but does not fully understand it. This is enough for salvation.

The second man is aware of the light of the sun, but having his eyes closed, can only see a glimmer of light through his eyelids. He represents a soul that is reformed in faith and feeling, and so is contemplative. Through grace he sees something of the Godhead of Jesus, but not clearly or fully. His eyelids, which may be likened to his bodily nature, act as a barrier between his nature and the nature of Jesus, and prevent him seeing clearly. By means of grace he penetrates the barrier and knows that Jesus is God: that he is sovereign goodness, sovereign being, and the source of all blessings. The soul sees all this by grace; and the purer and finer the soul becomes the less it is affected by bodily nature; its spiritual sight is sharper and its love of God greater. Such is the confidence of this soul, that even if no other person believed in and loved Jesus, its own love and faith would not lessen.

The third man, who sees the sun fully, has no need of faith, because his vision is clear. He represents a blessed soul whose sight is not obscured by the barriers of the body or sin, and who sees openly the face of Jesus in the bliss of heaven.

No soul can go beyond the second state in this life, for this is the state of perfection and the way to heaven.

How the gift of love, amongst all the gifts of Jesus, is the most worthy and profitable:

Ask nothing of God but the gift of love, which is the Holy Spirit. For all God's gifts there is none so good, so profitable, so worthy, so excellent as this. It is in this gift of love alone that God is both the giver and the gift.

How the secret voice of Jesus sounds in a soul, and how the enlightenment of the soul by grace may be called his voice:

The secret voice of Jesus is true, and it makes the soul true. There is no deception in it, nor pride, nor hypocrisy, but gentleness, peace, love and charity; it is full of life and grace. So when this voice speaks to a soul it may be so powerful that the soul puts aside what it is doing, whether it is praying, speaking, reading, thinking or working, and listens in rest and in love to the sweet sound of this spiritual voice. In this tranquility Jesus reveals himself to the soul, sometimes as a master to be feared, sometimes as a father to be respected and revered, and sometimes as a spouse to be loved. The soul becomes absorbed in a wonderful reverence that cannot be transcended. It feels secure and at deep rest, and desires only to remain in this state. It is in touch with the goodness of Jesus and by the grace of that touch it is made whole and safe, knowing Jesus alone. The only things it sees and feels are his goodness and favour.

This feeling can come without any special study of the Scriptures, and with few words at the mind's disposal, although the soul may use words to express the feelings of the heart. Because of this gracious feeling the soul is separated from the love of the world or any thought of it; it takes no heed of it.

Grace may bring certain enlightenment to the soul which I call the voice of Jesus, for it is the intention of Jesus to make the soul his perfect spouse. Because this cannot be done suddenly, Jesus in the wisdom of his love uses many wonderful ways to unite himself with his chosen soul. He woos it as a lover, he shows it his wonders and gives it precious gifts, always promising more and showing deep affection and courtesy.

The Ladder of Perfection

William Langland
1330–1386

Nothing is known about the author of Piers Ploughman *beyond what can be found in the text (which includes his signature in the form of a cryptogram). Three versions survive, which Langland must have spent much of his life revising. Long and sometimes rambling, the poem is arranged as a series of allegorical visions, most of which attack moral abuses in fourteenth-century church and society.*

A beautiful lady, clothed in linen, came down from a castle and called to me, saying: 'My son, are you asleep? You see these people and how they are milling about? Most people that pass through this life want nothing more than the world's praise; they never think of any other heaven than this.'

I was disturbed by something in her face, lovely though she was, and asked: 'Forgive me, Madam, but what does all this mean?'

'In the tower on the hill,' she said, 'lives Truth, and you would do well to follow his teaching. For he is father of Faith, who created you, giving you a body and a face and five senses to worship him with while you are here on earth. And he told the earth to give each of you wool and linen and food – as much as you need to live in comfort.

'And by his grace he provided three things for you to hold in common, and you need nothing but these so learn them well and list them in order and repeat them often. The first is clothing, to save you from the cold; the second is food, to spare you from misery; and the third is drink for when you are thirsty – and *only* then; do not drink too much so that you are the worse for it when you should be working.

'For it was through his weakness for drink that Lot followed the Devil's bidding with own daughters. Drawn by lechery he slept with them both while under the influence of drink – and then he blamed his wickedness on the wine.

' "Come," said his daughters, "let us make our father drink wine, and we will lie with him, that we may preserve the seed of our father."

'Thus through wine and through women Lot was overcome and in his drunkenness begat evil children. Therefore
shun sweet liquor and you will thrive. Moderation is better
for you, though you may yearn for more. Not everything your
stomach desires is good for your soul, nor are all the things
which nourish your soul food for your body. Don't believe
your body, for he's a liar tied to this evil world and would
betray you. The Devil and your body plot together to pursue
your soul and slay it in your heart. I advise you to be
wary.' . . .

Then I asked her politely, in the name of Him who created
her: 'What, madam, is the name of that gloomy castle deep
in the valley?'
  'That is the Castle of Care. Whoever enters there will
curse the day he was born. A creature called Wrong lives
there, the father of Falsehood. He built the place himself. It
was he who egged on Adam and Eve to sin; he persuaded
Cain to kill his brother; he deluded Judas with the Jews'
silver and afterwards hanged him on an elder tree. He gets
in the way of love and deceives everyone; those who put their
trust in his riches are the first to be betrayed.'
  Then I wondered who this woman was that I was talking
to, who displayed such wisdom over Holy Scripture. So before
she went, I asked her in the name of God who she was, who
taught me so kindly.
  'You ought to know who I am,' she replied. 'I am Holy
Church, who received you when you were a child and taught
you your faith. You pledged yourself to do my bidding and
to love me faithfully throughout your life.'
  Then I fell to my knees and cried out for mercy and
begged her piteously to pray for my sins. I asked her to teach
me plainly how to believe in Christ, who created me, that I
might do his will. 'Don't teach me about riches, Holy One –
just tell me this one thing: How can I save my soul?'

*[Here Holy Church tells the dreamer to hold fast to Truth, the greatest
treasure on earth:]*

'But I have no gift for grasping Truth,' I said. 'You must

teach me better. Do I have a special skill in my body for getting it, and if so, where is it?'

'You stupid oaf!' she retorted. 'How dull your wits are! You can't have learnt much Latin in your youth: *Heu mihi, quod sterilem duxi vitam iuvenilem!* ['Alas for my barren and misspent youth!']. It is your natural conscience which teaches your heart to love your Lord better than yourself and to die rather than commit a deadly sin.

'This is what I call Truth. If anyone can teach you better, let them try – then see what you think.

'For Truth tells that Love is Heaven's remedy [literally 'treacle'] and no stain of sin can be seen on anyone who uses this spice. It was through Love that God chose to perform all his works. He taught Moses that it was the dearest and most heavenly thing, and that it was also the plant of peace, its most precious property.

'Heaven could not hold Love it was so heavy, until it had fallen to earth and eaten its fill. But when it had assumed human flesh and blood, then no leaf on a linden tree could have been lighter. It was as swift and as piercing as the point of a needle, and no armour nor battlement could withstand it.

'Therefore Love is first within the Lord's company in heaven, and a mediator, as a mayor is between a king and the common people. In this way it is he who delivers judgement upon mankind for his misdeeds and he who sets the punishment.

'And so that you might recognise it by your inbuilt gifts, it springs up from the well at the centre of your heart by its own power. For each loving impulse begins with a natural instinct in your heart. That in turn comes from the Father who made us all, looked on us with love and let his innocent son die to pay for all our sins. And yet he wanted no evil to fall on those who tortured him and put him to death, but meekly prayed for Mercy to have pity on them . . .'

Piers Ploughman: (Passus 1, lines 2–42; 58–84; 136–169)

Julian of Norwich
c.1342–post-1416

Dame Julian lived as an anchoress in a cell attached to St Julian's Church in Norwich (hence her name). Her sixteen visions or 'shewings' came to her on 8 May 1373 after a near-fatal illness. She spent the next twenty years interpreting their meaning. Her writings portray a compassionate and homely deity – most notably where she talks about the motherhood of God – but her optimism is always a realistic one.

The First Revelation

Our Lord showed me a spiritual sight of his homely and familiar love. I saw that he is everything that is good and comforting to us; he is our clothing – wrapping and enfolding us. He embraces and encloses us in tender love, and he never leaves us. I saw that he is everything that is good, as I understand it.

He showed me a little thing, the size of a hazelnut, lying in the palm of my hand, as round as a ball. I looked at it and thought, 'What can this be?' And I was answered, 'It is all that is made.' I wondered how it could last, for I thought that being so small it might suddenly fall apart. And I was answered in my understanding, 'It lasts, and always will, because God loves it.' And so everything has its being through the love of God.

In this little thing I saw three properties. The first is that God made it; the second is that God loves it; the third is that God preserves it. But what is that to me? It is that God is the Creator, the lover and protector. For until I am united to him I cannot know love or rest or true happiness; that is, until I am so at one with him that no created thing can come between my God and me.

The Third Revelation

I saw God in a single point, and by this I knew that he is in all things. I gazed at it intently, knowing and understanding that God does all that is done. I marvelled at this sight with a gentle fear, and thought, 'What is sin?' For I saw in truth that God does everything, however small, and nothing is done by chance, but all by his all-seeing wisdom. If it seems like chance to us, it is because of our blindness and lack of foresight. For the things foreseen by God before time began and brought to their conclusion by him, come upon us suddenly and appear haphazard. In our blindness we say they are chance; but to God they are part of his infinite plan.

Through this revelation of love I understand that in our Lord's sight there is no chance; and I had to admit that, as our Lord does all, everything is done well. He is at the centre of everything and he does everything. And I was certain he does no sin!

The Seventh Revelation

Our Lord revealed to me a supreme spiritual pleasure in my soul. I was filled with the delight of everlasting assurance: I felt secure and without fear. This feeling was so welcome and precious to me that I felt totally rested and at peace: nothing on earth could have disturbed me.

But the delight was shortlived. It changed, and I felt abandoned and alone, oppressed and weary with myself, full of regrets with no patience or inclination to live. My only comfort was a memory of hope, faith and love, but truly I had no feeling of them. And then again our Lord gave me the delights of comfort, rest and security and my soul was free of fear and pain.

Soon, though, I was once more deeply disturbed and oppressed, and then peace and blessed delight returned. I turned from one to another again and again, perhaps twenty times. In the times of joy I might have said with St Paul, 'Nothing shall separate me from the love of Christ.' And when in pain I might have said with Peter, 'Lord, save me, I perish!'

This vision showed me that every man profits by such an experience: at times to be comforted, and at others to be bereft and left alone. God desires us to know that he keeps us safely and loves us fully at all times whether we are in sorrow or in joy.

The Thirteenth Revelation

Our Lord reminded me of the longing I had had for him before, and I saw that nothing hindered me but sin. I saw that it is the same for everyone, and it occurred to me that if there was no sin we should all be as pure as our Lord. Indeed, I had often wondered in the past why God had not prevented sin, for then all should have been well. Such thoughts were pride and folly on my part, and I should have left them alone. But our Lord, knowing my needs, informed me of all I needed to know saying, 'Sin is behovely; but all shall be well, and all shall be well, and all manner of thing shall be well.' . . .

These words were said to me so tenderly, without any hint of blame, so it would be ungracious of me to blame God or wonder at him because of my sin. And I glimpsed in these words something of the deep mystery of God which will be fully revealed to us in heaven for our endless joy, and which will show us why God allowed sin to be.

The Sixteenth Revelation

Our Lord opened my spiritual eye and showed me my soul in the middle of my heart. It was as vast as an entire kingdom. I understood it to be a fine city, with our Lord Jesus, true God and true man, seated in the middle, handsome and honourable and splendidly dressed. He sits in the soul, in peace and rest, and governs and protects everything in earth and heaven . . . He will never leave this place in our soul, for in us he has found his true home; and his greatest desire and pleasure is to remain there, and make it his eternal dwelling-place.

Our Lord's Meaning

From the time these things were revealed to me, I often wanted to know our Lord's meaning. Fifteen years later I was answered in my spiritual understanding. 'You wish to know our Lord's meaning in this thing? Know it well: love was his meaning. Who showed it to you? Love. What did he show you? Love. Why did he show it to you? For love. Stay with this and you shall know more of love.'

That was how I learned that love was our Lord's meaning.

And I saw without a doubt that before he created us, God loved us, and his love remains constant. All his works have been done in this love, and it is this love that gives us everlasting life. Our beginning was in our making, but the love which made us has no beginning: it is in this love that we have our beginning, and which we shall see in God without end.

Revelations of Divine Love

Geoffrey Chaucer
1343–1400

Chaucer doesn't content himself for long with this view of the ideal parson from the Prologue to the Canterbury Tales. *By the time he's halfway through his description the attack on typical clerical abuses is no longer under the surface. The point, of course, is that this shouldn't be an idealistic portrait but the norm.*

A good man was ther of religioun,
And was a povre PERSOUN of a town,
But riche he was of hooly thoght and werk.
He was also a lerned man, a clerk,
That Cristes gospel trewely wolde preche;
His parisshens devoutly wolde he teche,
Benygne he was, and wonder diligent,
And in adversitee ful pacient,
And swich he was ypreved ofte sithes.[1]
Ful looth were hym to cursen for his tithes,
But rather wolde he yeven,[2] out of doute,
Unto his povre parisshens aboute
Of his offrying and eek of his substaunce.
He koude in litel thyng have suffisaunce.
Wyd was his parisshe, and houses fer asonder,
But he ne lefte nat, for reyn ne thonder,
In siknesse nor in meschief to visite
The ferreste in his parisshe, muche and lite,
Upon his feet, and in his hand a staf.
This noble ensample to his sheep he yaf,

46

That first he wroghte, and afterward he taughte.
Out of the gospel he tho wordes caughte,
And this figure he added eek therto,
That if gold ruste, what shal iren do?
For if a preest be foul, on whom we truste,
No wonder is a lewed man to ruste;
And shame it is, if a prest take keep,
A shiten shepherde and a clene sheep.
Wel oghte a preest ensample for to yive,
By his clennesse, how that his sheep sholde lyve.
He sette nat his benefice to hyre
And leet his sheep encombred in the myre
And ran to Londoun unto Seinte Poules
To seken hym a chaunterie for soules,
Or with a bretherhed to been withholde;
But dwelte at hoom, and kepte wel his folde,
So that the wolf ne made it not myscarie;
He was a shepherde and noght a mercenarie.
And thogh he hooly were and vertuous,
He was to synful men nat despitous,[3]
Ne of his speche daungerous[4] ne digne,[5]
But in his techyng discreet and benygne.
To drawen folk to hevene by fairnesse,
By good ensample, this was his bisynesse.
But it were any persone obstinat,
What so he were, of heigh or lough estat,
Hym wolde he snybben[6] sharply for the nonys.
A bettre preest I trowe that nowher noon ys.
He waited after no pompe and reverence,
Ne maked him a spiced conscience,
But Christes loore and his apostles twelve
He taughte, but first he folwed it hymselve.

Prologue to the *Canterbury Tales*

1 so he was often proved   2 give   3 harsh   4 proud   5 scornful   6 rebuke

Margery Kempe
c.1373–1439

Seldom have the rôles of mystic and public nuisance been combined as they were in Margery Kempe. This independent and much travelled woman disturbed the townsfolk of Kings Lynn with her fits of wailing and shouting, and she succeeded in exasperating both archbishops, to whom she was taken as a supposed heretic. Her essentially orthodox and homely view of Christ was recognised by Julian of Norwich, however. (Her autobiography, the first in English, is written in the third person.)

After her child was born, she, not trusting to live, sent for her ghostly father . . . in full will to be shriven of all her lifetime, as near as she could. And when she came to the point for to say that thing which she had so long concealed, her confessor was a little too hasty and began sharply to reprove her, before she had fully said her intent, and so she would no more say for aught he might do. Anon, for the dread she had of damnation on the one side, and for his sharp reproving of her on the other side, this creature went out of her mind and was wondrously vexed and laboured with spirits for half a year, eight weeks and odd days.

And in this time she saw, as she thought, devils opening their mouths all inflamed with burning waves of fire, as if they would have swallowed her in, sometimes ramping at her, sometimes threatening her, pulling and hauling her, night and day during the aforesaid time. Also the devils cried upon her with great threatenings and bade her that she should forsake Christendom, her faith, and deny her God, His Mother and all the Saints in Heaven, her good works and all good virtues, her father, her mother and all her friends. And so she did. She slandered her husband, her friends and her own self. She said many a wicked word, and many a cruel word; she knew no virtue nor goodness; she desired all wickedness; like as the spirits tempted her to say and do, so she said and did. She would have destroyed herself many a time at their stirrings and have been damned with them in Hell, and in witness thereof, she bit her own hand so violently, that the mark was seen all her life after.

And also she rived the skin on her body against her heart with her nails spitefully, for she had no other instruments, and worse she would have done, but that she was bound and kept with strength day and night so that she might not have her will. And when she had long been laboured in these and many other temptations, so that men weened she would never have escaped or lived, then on a time as she lay alone and her keepers were from her, Our Merciful Lord Jesus Christ, ever to be trusted, worshipped be His Name, never forsaking His servant in time of need, appeared to His creature who had forsaken Him, in the likeness of a man, most seemly, most beauteous and most amiable that ever might be seen with man's eye, clad in a mantle of purple silk, sitting upon her bedside, looking upon her with so blessed a face that she was strengthened in all her spirit, and said to her these words: 'Daughter, why hast thou forsaken Me, and I forsook never thee?'

And anon, as He said these words, she saw verily how the air opened as bright as any lightning. And he rose up into the air, not right hastily and quickly, but fair and easily, so that she might well behold Him in the air till it was closed again.

And anon this creature became calmed in her wits and reason, as well as ever she was before, and prayed her husband as soon as he came to her, that she might have the keys of the buttery to take her meat and drink as she had done before. Her maidens and her keepers counselled him that he should deliver her no keys, as they said she would but give away such goods as there were, for she knew not what she said, as they weened.

Nevertheless, her husband ever having tenderness and compassion for her, commanded that they should deliver to her the keys; and she took her meat and drink as her bodily strength would serve her, and knew her friends and her household and all others that came to see how Our Lord Jesus Christ had wrought His grace in her, so blessed may He be, Who ever is near in tribulation . . .

Another time, as she prayed to God that she might live chaste by leave of her husband, Christ said to her:

'Thou must fast on Friday, both from meat and drink, and thou shalt have thy desire ere Whitsunday, for I shall suddenly slay (the fleshly lust in) thy husband.'

Then on the Wednesday in Easter week, after her husband would have had knowledge of her, as he was wont before, and when he came nigh to her, she said: 'Jesus Christ, help me,' and he had no power to touch her at that time in that way, nor ever after with any fleshly knowledge . . .

Then she was bidden by Our Lord to go to an anchoress in the same city, named Dame Jelyan [Julian of Norwich], and so she did, and showed her the grace that God put into her soul, of compunction, contrition, sweetness and devotion, compassion with holy meditation and high contemplation, and full many holy speeches and dalliance that Our Lord spake to her soul; and many wonderful revelations, which she shewed to the anchoress to find out if there were any deceit in them, for the anchoress was expert in such things, and good counsel could give.

The anchoress, hearing the marvellous goodness of Our Lord, highly thanked God with all her heart for His visitation, counselling this creature to be obedient to the will of Our Lord God and to fulfil with all her might whatever He put into her soul, if it were not against the worship of God, and profit of her fellow Christians, for if it were, then it were not the moving of a good spirit, but rather of an evil spirit. 'The Holy Ghost moveth ne'er a thing against charity, for if He did, He would be contrary to His own self for He is all charity. Also He moveth a soul to all chasteness, for chaste livers are called to the Temple of the Holy Ghost, and the Holy Ghost maketh a soul stable and steadfast in the right faith, and the right belief.

'And a double man in soul is ever unstable and unsteadfast in all his ways. He that is ever doubting is like the flood of the sea which is moved and borne about with the wind, and that man is not likely to receive the gifts of God.

'Any creature that hath these tokens may steadfastly believe that the Holy Ghost dwelleth in his soul.'

First when she had her cryings in Jerusalem, she had them

often, and in Rome also. And when she came home to England, first at her coming home, it came but seldom, as it were once a month, then once a week, afterwards daily, and once she had fourteen in one day, and another day she had seven, and so on, as God would visit her, sometimes in church, sometimes in the street, sometimes in her chamber, sometimes in the fields, whenever God would send them, for she never knew the time nor the hour when they would come. And they never came without passing great sweetness of devotion and high contemplation.

And as soon as she perceived that she would cry, she would keep it in as much as she might that the people should not hear it, to their annoyance. For some said that a wicked spirit vexed her; some said it was a sickness; some said she had drunk too much wine; some banned her; some wished she was in the harbour; some wished she was on the sea in a bottomless boat; and thus each man as he thought. Other ghostly men loved her and favoured her the more. Some great clerks said Our Lady cried never so, nor any saint in Heaven, but they knew full little what she felt, nor would they believe that she could not stop crying if she wished.

She had as very contemplation in the sight of her soul, as if Christ had hung before her bodily eye in His Manhood. And when through the dispensation of the high mercy of Our Sovereign Saviour Christ Jesus, it was granted to this creature to behold so verily His precious tender body, all rent and torn with scourges, fuller of wounds than ever was a dove-house of holes, hanging on the Cross with the crown of thorns upon His head, His beautiful hands, His tender feet nailed to the hard tree, the rivers of blood flowing out plenteously from every member, the grisly and grievous wound in His precious side shedding blood and water for her love and her salvation, then she fell down and cried with a loud voice, wonderfully turning and wresting her body on every side, spreading her arms abroad as if she would have died, and could not keep herself from crying, and from these bodily movements for the fire of love that burnt so fervently in her soul with pure pity and compassion.

The Book of Margery Kempe

'Adam Lay Ibounden'
15th century

What appears an attractive but twisted piece of logical thought was in fact taken seriously by medieval theologians (despite Paul's warning in his letter to the Romans). Called 'Felix culpa' the argument runs that sin is a good thing since it draws forth more grace and forgiveness from God. This and the next lyric show how much veneration the English had for Mary at this time.

Adam lay ibounden,
    Bounden in a bond;
Foure thousand winter
    Thought he not too long.

And all was for an apple,
    An apple that he tok,
As clerkes finden
    Wreten in here[1] book.

Ne hadde the apple take ben,
    The apple taken ben,
Ne hadde never our lady
    A-ben hevene quen.

Blissed be the time
    That apple take was.
Therefore we moun singen
    Deo gracias!

1 their

'I Sing of a Maiden'

15th century

I sing of a maiden
That is makeles:[1]
King of alle kinges
To here sone she ches.[2]

He cam also stille
Ther his moder was,
As dew in Aprille
That falleth on the grass.

He cam also stille
To his moderes bowr,
As dew in Aprille
That falleth on the flowr.

He cam also stille
Ther his moder lay,
As dew in Aprille
That falleth on the spray.

Moder and maiden:
Was never non but she:
Well may swich a lady
Godes moder be.

1 matchless   2 she chose for her son

'Lully, Lulley, Lully, Lulley'
late 15th century

This is one of the lyrics which draws on chivalric romance for its imagery. The result is startling, with the mysterious figure of the falcon and Mary cast in the rôle of the knight's lover.

Lully, lulley, lully, lulley!
The fawcon[1] hath borne my mak[2] away.

He bare him up, he bare him down,
He bare him in to an orchard brown.
Lully, lulley, lully, lulley,
The fawcon hath borne my mak away.

In that orchard ther was an hall,
That was hanged with purpill and pall.
Lully, lulley, lully, lulley,
The fawcon hath borne my mak away.

And in that hall ther was a bed,
It was hanged with gold so red.
Lully, lulley, lully, lulley,
The fawcon hath borne my mak away.

And in that bed ther lythe a knight,
His woundes bleeding day and night.
Lully, lulley, lully, lulley,
The fawcon hath borne my mak away.

By that bedes side kneleth a may,[3]
And she wepeth both night and day.
Lully, lulley, lully, lulley,
The fawcon hath borne my mak away.

And by that bedes side ther stondeth a stone,
Corpus Christi wreten thereon.
Lully, lulley, lully, lulley,
The fawcon hath borne my mak away.

1 falcon   2 mate   3 maiden

'My Dancing Day'
15th century?

This has been described as 'the most audacious' of the medieval ballad carols because of its fusion of sacred and secular love and its sheer exuberance. Nothing is known about the earliest forms of 'My Dancing Day'; this version was published in 1833, together with the popular melody.

Tomorrow shall be my dancing day:
    I would my true love did so chance
To see the legend of my play,
    To call my true love to my dance:

Sing O my love, O my love, my love, my love;
This have I done for my true love.

Then was I born of a virgin pure,
    Of her I took fleshly substance;
Thus was I knit to man's nature,
    To call my true love to my dance:

In a manger laid and wrapped I was,
    So very poor, this was my chance,
Betwixt an ox and a silly poor ass,
    To call my true love to my dance:

Then afterwards baptized I was;
    The Holy Ghost on me did glance,
My Father's voice heard from above,
    To call my true love to my dance:

Into the desert I was led,
    Where I fasted without substance;
The devil bade me make stones my bread,
    To have me break my true love's dance:

The Jews on me they made great suit,
    And with me made great variance,
Because they loved darkness rather than light,
    To call my true love to my dance:

For thirty pence Judas me sold,
    His covetousness for to advance;
'Mark whom I kiss, the same do hold,'
    The same is he shall lead the dance:

Before Pilate the Jews me brought,
    Where Barabbas had deliverance;
They scourged me and set me at nought,
    Judged me to die to lead the dance:

Then on the cross hanged I was,
    Where a spear to my heart did glance;
There issued forth both water and blood,
    To call my true love to my dance:

Then down to hell I took my way
    For my true love's deliverance,
And rose again on the third day,
    Up to my true love and the dance:

Then up to heaven I did ascend,
    Where now I dwell in sure substance,
On the right hand of God, that man
    May come unto the general dance:

'Everyman'
c.1509–1519

One of the later and certainly the most popular of the medieval morality plays, which, together with the mysteries, supplemented the Latin church services and laid the foundations for Elizabethan drama.

Everyman comes to his grave:

EVERYMAN: Alas, I am so faint I may not stand;
                My limbs under me doth fold.
                Friends, let us not turn again to this land,
                Not for all the world's gold;
                For into this cave must I creep
                And turn to earth, and there to sleep.

BEAUTY:	What, into this grave? Alas!
EVERYMAN:	Yea, there shall ye consume, more and less.
BEAUTY:	And what, should I smother here?
EVERYMAN:	Yea, by my faith, and never more appear.
	In this world live no more we shall,
	But in heaven before the highest Lord of all.
BEAUTY:	I cross out all this; adieu, by Saint John!
	I take my cap in my lap, and am gone.
EVERYMAN:	What, Beauty, whither will ye?
BEAUTY:	Peace, I am deaf; I look not behind me,
	Not and thou wouldest give me all the gold in thy chest.

                                                [Exit BEAUTY]

EVERYMAN:	Alas, whereto may I trust?
	Beauty goeth fast away from me;
	She promised with me to live and die.
STRENGTH:	Everyman, I will thee also forsake and deny;
	Thy game liketh[1] me not at all.
EVERYMAN:	Why, then, ye will forsake me all?
	Sweet Strength, tarry a little space.[2]
STRENGTH:	Nay, sir, by the rood of grace!
	I will hie me from thee fast,
	Though thou weep till thy heart to-brast.[3]
EVERYMAN:	Ye would ever bide by me, ye said.
STRENGTH:	Yea, I have you far enough conveyed.
	Ye be old enough, I understand,
	Your pilgrimage to take on hand;
	I repent me that I hither came.
EVERYMAN:	Strength, you to displease I am to blame;
	Yet promise is debt, this ye well wot.
STRENGTH:	In faith, I care not.
	Thou art but a fool to complain;
	You spend your speech and waste your brain.
	Go thrust thee into the ground!

                                              [Exit STRENGTH]

EVERYMAN:	I had wend surer I should you have found.
	Him that trusteth in his Strength
	She him deceiveth at the length.

1 pleases   2 while   3 break

	Both Strength and Beauty forsaketh me;
	Yet they promised me fair and lovingly.
DISCRETION:	Everyman, I will after Strength be gone;
	As for me, I will leave you alone.
EVERYMAN:	Why, Discretion, will ye forsake me?
DISCRETION:	Yea, in faith, I will go from thee,
	For when Strength goeth before
	I follow after evermore.
EVERYMAN:	Yet, I pray thee, for the love of the Trinity,
	Look in my grave once piteously.
DISCRETION:	Nay, so nigh will I not come;
	Farewell, every one!

[*Exit* DISCRETION]

EVERYMAN:	O, all thing faileth, save God alone –
	Beauty, Strength and Discretion;
	For when Death bloweth his blast,
	They all run from me full fast.
FIVE WITS:	Everyman, my leave now of thee I take;
	I will follow the other, for here I thee forsake.
EVERYMAN:	Alas, then may I wail and weep,
	For I took you for my best friend.
FIVE WITS:	I will no longer thee keep;
	Now farewell, and there an end.

[*Exit* FIVE WITS]

EVERYMAN:	O Jesu, help! All hath forsaken me.
GOOD DEEDS:	Nay, Everyman; I will bide with thee.
	I will not forsake thee indeed;
	Thou shalt find me a good friend at need.
EVERYMAN:	Gramercy, Good Deeds! Now may I true
	friends see.
	They have forsaken me, every one;
	I loved them better than my Good Deeds
	alone.
	Knowledge, will ye forsake me also?
KNOWLEDGE:	Yea, Everyman, when ye to Death shall go;
	But not yet, for no manner of danger.
EVERYMAN:	Gramercy, Knowledge, with all my heart.
KNOWLEDGE:	Nay, yet I will not from hence depart
	Till I see where ye shall become.
EVERYMAN:	Methink, alas, that I must be gone

	To make my reckoning and my debts pay,
	For I see my time is nigh sped away.
	Take example, all ye that this do hear or see,
	How they that I loved best do forsake me,
	Except my Good Deeds that bideth truly.
GOOD DEEDS:	All earthly things is but vanity:
	Beauty, Strength, and Discretion do men forsake,
	Foolish friends, and kinsmen, that fair spake –
	All fleeth save Good Deeds, and that am I.
EVERYMAN:	Have mercy on me, God most mighty;
	And stand by me, thou mother and maid, holy Mary.
GOOD DEEDS:	Fear not; I will speak for thee.
EVERYMAN:	Here I cry God mercy.
GOOD DEEDS:	Short[1] our end, and minish[2] our pain;
	Let us go and never come again.
EVERYMAN:	Into thy hands, Lord, my soul I commend;
	Receive it, Lord, that it be not lost.
	As thou me boughtest, so me defend,
	And save me from the fiend's boast,
	That I may appear with that blessed host
	That shall be saved at the day of doom,
	In manus tuas, of mights most
	For ever, *commendo spiritum meum*.

[He sinks into his grave]

KNOWLEDGE:	Now hath he suffered that we all shall endure;
	The Good Deeds shall make all sure.
	Now hath he made ending;
	Methinketh that I hear angels sing,
	And make great joy and melody
	Where Everyman's soul received shall be.
ANGEL:	Come, excellent elect spouse, to Jesu!
	Hereabove thou shalt go
	Because of thy singular virtue.
	Now the soul is taken the body fro,
	Thy reckoning is crystal-clear.
	Now shalt thou into the heavenly sphere,
	Unto the which all ye shall come
	That liveth well before the day of doom.

1 shorten   2 diminish

Sir Thomas More
1478–1535

More did not always practise the religious tolerance he preached in
Utopia, *his Platonic critique of sixteenth-century Europe. As Lord
Chancellor, he reluctantly but diligently followed the Church's teaching
that unrepentant heretics were better burnt. A loving family man, who
had at one time thought of becoming a priest, he was executed in his
turn for resisting Henry VIII's divorce.*

There be diverse kinds of religion, not only in sundry parts
of the Island, but also in diverse places of every city. Some
worship for God the sun; some the moon; some some other
of the planets. There be them that give worship to a man
that was once of excellent virtue or of famous glory, not only
as God, but also as the chiefest and highest God. But the
most and the wisest part (rejecting all this) believe that there
is a certain Godly power unknown, everlasting, incomprehensible, inexplicable, far above the capacity and reach of man's
wit, dispersed through out all the world, not in bigness, but
in virtue and power. Him they call the father of all . . .

But after they heard us speak of the name of Christ, of
his doctrine, laws, miracles, and of the no less wonderful
constancy of so many martyrs, whose blood willingly shed
brought a great number of nations through out all parts of
the world into their sect; you will not believe with how glad
minds they agreed unto the same; whether it were by the
secret inspiration of God, or else for that they thought it next
unto that opinion which among them is counted chiefest.
How it be, I think this was no small help and furtherance in
the matter, that they heard us say that Christ instituted
among his all things common; and that the same community
doth yet remain amongst the rightest Christian companies.
Verily, howsoever it came to pass, many of them consented
together in our religion, and were washed in the holy water
of baptism . . .

They also, which do not agree to Christ's religion, fear no
man from it, nor speak against any man that hath received

60

it. Saving that one of our company in my presence was sharply punished. He, as soon as he was baptised, began against our wills, with more earnest affection than wisdom, to reason of Christ's religion; and began to wax so hot in his matter, that he did not only prefer our religion before all other, but also did utterly despise and condemn all other, calling them profane, and the followers of them wicked and devilish, and the children of everlasting damnation. When he had thus long reasoned the matter, they laid hold on him, accused him, and condemned him into exile; not as a despiser of religion, but as a seditious person, and a raiser up of dissension among the people. For this is one of the ancientest laws among them: that no man shall be blamed for reasoning in the maintenance of his own religion.

They be divided into two sects. The one is of them that live single and chaste, abstaining not only from the company of women, but also from the eating of flesh, and some of them from all manner of beasts. Which, utterly rejecting the pleasures of this present life as hurtful, be all wholly set upon the desire of the life to come; by watching and sweating hoping shortly to obtain it, being in the mean season merry and lusty. The other sect is no less desirous of labour, but they embrace matrimony; not despising the solace thereof; thinking that they can not be discharged of their bounden duties towards nature without labour and toil nor towards their native country, without procreation of children. They abstain from no pleasure that doth nothing hinder them from labour. They love the flesh of four footed beasts, because they believe that by that meat they be made hardier and stronger to work. The Utopians count this sect the wiser, but the other the holier . . .

Utopia

Trust well in God and he shall provide you outward teachers suitable for every time, or else shall himself sufficiently teach you inwardly.

VINCENT: . . . I can see no good man praying God to send another sorrow, nor are there such prayers put in the priests' breviaries, as far as I can hear. And yet if it were as you say, good uncle, that perpetual prosperity were so perilous to the soul, and tribulation also so fruitful, then meseemeth every man would be bound of charity not only to pray God send his neighbour sorrow, but also to help thereto himself. And when folk were sick, they would be bound not to pray God send them health, but when they came to comfort them, they should say, 'I am glad, good friend, that you are so sick – I pray God keep you long therein!' And neither should any man give any medicine to another nor take any medicine himself neither. For by the diminishing of the tribulation he taketh away part of the profit from his soul, which can with no bodily profit be sufficiently recompensed.

ANTHONY: I think indeed tribulation so good and profitable that I might doubt, as you do, why a man might labour and pray to be delivered of it, were it not that God, who teacheth us the one, teacheth us also the other. For as he biddeth us take our pain patiently, and exhort our neighbours to do also the same, so biddeth he us also not forbear to do our best to remove the pain from us both. And then, since it is God who teacheth both, I shall not need to break my brain in devising wherefore he would bid us to do both, the one seeming opposed to the other . . . Fasting is better than eating, and hath more thanks of God, and yet will God that we shall eat. Praying is better than drinking, and much more pleasing to God, and yet will God that we shall drink. Keeping vigil is much more acceptable to God than sleeping, and yet will God that we shall sleep. God hath given us our bodies here to keep, and will that we maintain them to do him service with, till he send for us hence.

Dialogue of Comfort against Tribulation

Give me, good Lord, a full faith, a firm hope; and a fervent charity, a love to Thee, good Lord, incomparable above the love to myself, and that I love nothing to Thy displeasure, but everything in an order to Thee.

Give me, good Lord, a longing to be with Thee, not for the avoiding of the calamities of this wretched world, nor so much for the avoiding of the pains of purgatory, nor of the pains of hell neither, nor so much for the attaining of the joys of heaven, in respect of mine own commodity, as even for a very love to Thee.

And bear me, good Lord, Thy love and favour, which thing my love to Thee-ward (were it never so great) could not but of Thy great goodness deserve.

Lord, give me patience in tribulation, and grace in everything to conform my will to Thine . . . The things, good Lord, that I pray for, give me the grace to labour for.

Prayers

Thomas Cranmer
1489–1556

Thomas Cranmer was the guiding spirit of the English Reformation, and was the main compiler of the Book of Common Prayer. He became Archbishop of Canterbury under Henry VIII and was in fact a relatively conservative churchman. His reform of the English Church grew out of his reading of the New Testament and the need to remove abuses, rather than from a radical zeal. This was not appreciated by the Catholic Queen Mary, who had him burnt as a heretic. (See also The Book of Common Prayer).

His Prayer before Death

O Father of heaven; O Son of God, Redeemer of the world; O Holy Ghost, proceeding from them both; three Persons, and one God; have mercy upon me, most wretched caitiff and miserable sinner. I have offended both heaven and earth, more grievously than any tongue can express. Whither then may I go, or whither should I flee for succour? To heaven I may be ashamed to lift up mine eyes, and in earth I find no refuge or succour. What shall I then do? Shall I despair? God forbid. O good God, thou art merciful, and refusest none that cometh unto Thee for succour. To Thee, therefore, do I run; to Thee do I humble myself; saying, O Lord God, my sins be great, but yet have mercy upon me for thy great mercy. O God the Son, this great mystery was not wrought (that God became man) for few or small offences; nor Thou didst

not give thy Son unto death, O God the Father, for our little
and small sins only, but for all the greatest sins of the world,
so that the sinner return unto Thee with a penitent heart, as
I do here at this present. Wherefore have mercy upon me, O
Lord, whose property is always to have mercy; for although
my sins be great, yet thy mercy is greater. And I crave
nothing, O Lord, for mine own merits, but for thy name's
sake, that it may be glorified thereby, and for thy dear Son,
Jesus Christ's sake.

His Exhortation before Death

Every man, good people, desireth at the time of his death to
give some good exhortation, that others may remember the
same before their death, and be the better thereby: so I
beseech God grant me grace, that I may speak something at
this my departing, whereby God may be glorified, and you
edified.

First, it is an heavy case to see that so many folk so much
doat upon the love of this false world, and be so careful for
it, that of the love of God, or the world to come, they seem
to care very little or nothing. Therefore this shall be my first
exhortation, that you set not your minds over much upon this
glozing world, but upon God and upon the world to come;
and to learn to know what this lesson meaneth which St John
teacheth, that *the love of this world is hatred against God.*

The second exhortation is, that next under God you obey
your King and Queen, willingly and gladly, without mur-
muring or grudging: not for fear of them only, but much more
for the fear of God; knowing that they be God's ministers,
appointed by God to rule and govern you; and therefore
whosoever resisteth them, resisteth the ordinance of God.

The third exhortation is, that you love altogether like
brethren and sisters. For, alas! pity it is to see what contention
and hatred one Christian man beareth to another; not taking
each other as brother and sister, but rather as strangers and
mortal enemies. But, I pray you, learn and bear well away
this one lesson, to do good unto all men, as much as in you
lieth, and to hurt no man, no more than you would hurt your
own natural loving brother or sister. For this you may be

sure of, that whosoever hateth any person, and goeth about maliciously to hinder or hurt him, surely, and without all doubt, God is not with that man, although he think himself never so much in God's favour.

John Foxe
1516–1587

With Foxe's Book of Martyrs *almost compulsory Sunday reading for the next 300 years (along with* Pilgrim's Progress*) it is no wonder that the Reformation wounds have been slow to heal. Writing in exile on the continent, Foxe, though personally remarkably tolerant, was not exactly a neutral historian. But then, martyrology has never been a neutral subject.*

Rowland Taylor, Vicar of Hadleigh, Suffolk.
[Arrested in London. Burned on Aldham Common in his own parish, 1555]

Now when the Sheriff and his company came against St Botolph's Church, Elizabeth cried, saying, 'O my dear Father! Mother! Mother! here is my father led away.' Then cried his wife, 'Rowland, Rowland, where art thou?' – for it was a very dark morning, that the one could not well see the other. Dr Taylor answered, 'Dear wife, I am here,' and stayed. The Sheriff's men would have led him forth, but the Sheriff said, 'Stay a little, masters, I pray you, and let him speak with his wife,' and so they stayed. Then came she to him, and he took his daughter Mary in his arms, and he, his wife and Elizabeth kneeled down and said the Lord's Prayer. At which sight the Sheriff wept apace, and so did divers other of the company. After they had prayed he rose up and kissed his wife and shook her by the hand, and said, 'Farewell, my dear wife, be of good comfort, for I am quiet in my conscience. God shall stir up a father for my children.' . . . Then said his wife, 'God be with thee, dear Rowland. I will with God's grace meet thee at Hadleigh . . .' All the way Dr Taylor was joyful and merry as one that accounteth himself going to a most pleasant banquet or bridal . . . Coming within a two mile of Hadleigh he desired to light off his horse, which done he leaped and set a frisk or twain, as men commonly do in dancing. 'Why, master Doctor,' quoth the Sheriff, 'how do you now?' He answered, 'Well, God be praised, good master Sheriff, never better; for now I know I am almost at home. I lack not past two stiles to go over, and I am even at my Father's house.'

The Execution of Bishops Latimer and Ridley, 1555

. . . When every thing was in a readiness, the prisoners were brought forth by the mayor and the bailiffs. Master Ridley had a fair black gown furred, and faced with foins, such as he was wont to wear being bishop, and a tippet of velvet furred likewise about his neck, a velvet nightcap upon his head, and a corner cap upon the same, going in a pair of slippers to the stake, and going between the mayor and an alderman, etc.

After him came master Latimer in a poor Bristow frieze frock all worn, with his buttoned cap, and a kerchief on his head all ready to the fire, a new long shroud hanging over his hose down to the feet; which at the first sight stirred men's hearts to rue upon them, beholding on the one side the honour they sometime had, and on the other, the calamity whereunto they were fallen . . .

Then master Ridley, looking back, espied master Latimer coming after, unto whom he said, 'Oh, be ye there?' 'Yea,' said master Latimer, 'have after as fast as I can follow.' So he following a pretty way off, at length they came both to the stake, the one after the other, where first Dr Ridley entering the place, marvellous earnestly holding up both his hands, looked towards heaven. Then shortly after espying master Latimer, with a wondrous cheerful look he ran to him, embraced and kissed him; and, as they that stood near reported, comforted him saying, 'Be of good heart, brother, for God will either assuage the fury of the flame, or else strengthen us to abide it.' With that went he to the stake, kneeled down by it, kissed it, and most effectuously prayed, and behind him master Latimer kneeled, as earnestly calling upon God as he . . .

Incontinently they were commanded to make them ready,

which they with all meekness obeyed. Master Ridley took his gown and his tippet, and gave it to his brother-in-law master Shepside . . . Master Latimer gave nothing, but very quickly suffered his keeper to pull off his hose, and his other array, which to look unto was very simple; and being stripped into his shroud, he seemed as comely a person to them that were there present as one should lightly see; and whereas in his clothes he appeared a withered and crooked silly old man, he now stood bolt upright, as comely a father as one might lightly behold.

Then master Ridley, standing as yet in his truss, said to his brother: 'It were best for me to go in my truss still.' 'No,' quoth his brother, 'it will put you to more pain; and the truss will do a poor man good.' Whereunto master Ridley said: 'Be it, in the name of God;' and so unlaced himself . . .

Then the smith took a chain of iron, and brought the same about both Dr Ridley's and master Latimer's middles; and as he was knocking in a staple, Dr Ridley took the chain in his hand, and shaked the same, for it did gird his belly, and looking aside to the smith, said: 'Good fellow, knock it in hard, for the flesh will have his course . . .'

Then they brought a fagot, kindled with fire, and laid the same down at Dr Ridley's feet. To whom master Latimer spake in this manner: 'Be of good comfort, master Ridley, and play the man. We shall this day light such a candle, by God's grace, in England, as I trust shall never be put out.'

History of the Acts and Monuments of the Christian Martyrs and Matters Ecclesiastical passed in the Church of Christ from the Primitive Beginning to these our Days, as well in other Countries as namely in England and Scotland (known as Foxe's Book of Martyrs)

The Book of Common Prayer
1549

It is impossible to over-stress the importance of Cranmer's Prayer Book to the development of English spirituality. It typifies the Anglican via media *and yet it is in no way a document of compromise. Cranmer's prime achievement was his successful adaptation of England's traditional monastic liturgy – such as the daily office and frequent communion – to the needs of the whole Church.*

Collect for Peace (Matins)

O God, which art author of peace, and lover of concord, in knowledge of whom standeth our eternal life, whose service is perfect freedom: defend us, thy humble servants, in all assaults of our enemies, that we, surely trusting in thy defence, may not fear the power of any adversaries: through the might of Jesu Christ our Lord.

Collect for Grace (Matins)

O Lord, our heavenly Father, almighty and everliving God, which hast safely brought us to the beginning of this day: defend us in the same with thy mighty power; and grant that this day we fall into no sin, neither run into any kind of danger, but that all our doings may be ordered by thy governance, to do always that is righteous in thy sight: through Jesus Christ our Lord.

Second Collect (Evensong)

O God, from whom all holy desires, all good counsels, and all just works do proceed: Give unto thy servants that peace which the world cannot give; that both our hearts may be set to obey thy commandments, and also that by thee we, being defended from the fear of our enemies, may pass our time in rest and quietness: through the merits of Jesu Christ our Saviour.

Collect for Aid against all Perils (Evensong)

Lighten our darkness, we beseech thee, O Lord, and by thy great mercy, defend us from all perils and dangers of this night, for the love of thy only Son, our Saviour Jesu Christ.

Collect for Purity (Holy Communion)

Almighty God, unto whom all hearts be open, and all desires known, and from whom no secrets are hid: cleanse the thoughts of our hearts, by the inspiration of thy Holy Spirit: that we may perfectly love thee, and worthily magnify thy holy name: through Christ our Lord.

Prayer of Humble Access (Holy Communion)

We do not presume to come to this thy table (O merciful Lord) trusting in our own righteousness, but in thy manifold and great mercies: we be not worthy so much as to gather up the crumbs under thy table. but thou art the same Lord whose property is always to have mercy: Grant us therefore (gracious Lord) so to eat the flesh of thy dear Son Jesus Christ, and to drink his blood in these holy Mysteries, that we may continually dwell in him, and he in us, that our sinful bodies may be made clean by his body, and our souls washed through his most precious blood.

Collect for Quinquagesima

O Lord, which dost teach us that all our doings without charity are nothing worth: send thy Holy Ghost, and pour into our heart that most excellent gift of charity, the very bond of peace and all virtues, without the which, whosoever liveth is counted dead before thee: Grant this, for thy only son Jesus Christ's sake.

Collect for the fourth Sunday after Easter

Almighty God, which dost make the minds of all faithful men to be of one will: grant unto thy people, that they may love the thing, which thou commandest, and desire that which thou dost promise, that among the sundry and manifold changes of the world, our hearts may surely there be fixed, whereas true joys are to be found: through Christ our Lord.

Collect for the fifth Sunday after Easter

Lord, from whom all good things do come; grant us thy humble servants, that by thy holy inspiration we may think those things that be good, and by thy merciful guiding may perform the same: through our Lord Jesus Christ.

Collect for the sixth Sunday after Trinity Sunday

God, which hast prepared to them that love thee, such good things as pass all man's understanding: Pour into our hearts such love toward thee, that we loving thee in all things, may obtain thy promises, which exceed all that we can desire: through Jesus Christ our Lord.

Collect for St Michael and all Angels

Everlasting God, which hast ordained and constituted the services of all Angels and men in a wonderful order: mercifully grant, that they which alway do thee service in heaven, may by thy appointment succour and defend us in earth: through Jesus Christ our Lord.

Sir Philip Sidney
1554–1586

The prayer of the imprisoned and tortured Princess Pamela from Sidney's Arcadia *was a favourite of King Charles I, whom Milton reproached for 'having stolen a prayer word for word from the mouth of a heathen woman praying to a heathen god'. Strictly speaking he was right but, under the guise of a classical landscape, Sidney was portraying Elizabethan England.*

O all-seeing Light and eternal Life of all things, to whom nothing is either so great, that it may resist; or so small, that it is condemned; look upon my misery with thine eye of mercy, and let thine infinite power vouchsafe to limit out some proportion of deliverance unto me, as to thee shall seem most convenient. Let not injury, O Lord, triumph over me, and let my faults by thy hands be corrected, and make not mine unjust enemy the minister of thy Justice. But yet, my

God, if in thy wisdom this be the aptest chastizement for my inexcusable folly; if this low bondage be fittest for my over-high desires; if the pride of my not-enough humble heart be thus to be broken, O Lord, I yield unto thy will, and joyfully embrace what sorrow thou wilt have me suffer. Only thus much let me crave of thee (let my craving, O Lord, be accepted of thee, since even that proceeds from thee), let me crave, even by the noblest title, which in my greatest affliction I may give my self, that I am thy creature, and by thy goodness (which is thyself) that thou wilt suffer some beam of thy Majesty so to shine into my mind, that it may still depend confidently upon thee. Let calamity be the exercise but not the overthrow of my virtue: let their power prevail, but prevail not to destruction: let my greatness be their prey: let my pain be the sweetness of their revenge: let them (if so it seem good unto thee) vex me with more and more punishment. But, O Lord, let never their wickedness have such a hand, but that I may carry a pure mind in a pure body . . .

Arcadia (Book Three)

Richard Hooker
1554–1600

In the religious divisions of Queen Elizabeth's reign Richard Hooker sought a middle way between Catholics and Puritans. His Laws of Ecclesiastical Polity *is a masterpiece of theology and political philosophy, affirming that the Anglican Church is based equally on the Bible, Tradition and Reason.*

Zeal, unless it be rightly guided, when it endeavoureth most busily to please God, forceth upon him those unseasonable offices which please him not . . . Zeal, except it be ordered aright, when it bendeth itself unto conflict with things either in deed, or but imagined to be opposite unto religion, useth the razor many times with such eagerness, that the very life of religion itself is thereby hazarded; through hatred of tares the corn in the field of God is plucked up. So that zeal needeth both ways a sober guide.

71

Fear on the other side, if it have not the light of true understanding concerning God, wherewith to be moderated, breedeth likewise superstition. It is therefore dangerous, that in things divine we should work too much upon the spur either of zeal or fear.

We admire the goodness of God in nature, when we consider how he hath provided that things most needful to preserve this life should be most prompt and easy for all living creatures to come by. Is it not as evident a sign of his wonderful providence over us, when that food of eternal life, upon the *utter want* whereof our endless death and destruction necessarily ensueth, is prepared and always set in such a readiness, that those very means than which nothing is more easy may suffice to procure the same? Surely if we perish it is not the lack of scribes and learned expounders that can be our just excuse. The word which saveth our souls is near us; we need for knowledge but to read and live. The man which readeth the word of God the word itself doth pronounce blessed, if he also observe the same.

Of the Laws of Ecclesiastical Polity

Lancelot Andrewes
1555–1626

Andrewes was Bishop of Ely and then of Winchester and his advice was sought by Elizabeth I, James I and Charles I. A moderate force in religious politics, his more particular contribution was to root Anglicanism in the teaching of the Early Fathers. He was among those who produced the Authorized Version of the Bible.

The Comforter Will Come

Our manner is, we love to be left to ourselves in our consultations, to advise with flesh and blood; thence to take our direction all our life: and, when we must part, then send for Him, for a little comfort and there is all the use we have of Him. But, he that will have comfort from Him, must also take counsel of Him; have use of Him as well against error and sinful life, as against heaviness of mind. If not, here is your doom: where you have had your counsel, there seek your comfort: he that hath been your counsellor all the time of your life, let him be your comforter at the hour of your death.

Sermon Four on the Holy Ghost: Whit Sunday 1611

Turn You unto Me

Repentance itself is nothing else but a kind of circling; to return to Him by repentance, from whom by sin we have turned away . . . which circle consists of two things; which two must needs be two different motions. One, is to be done with the whole heart; the other with it broken and rent: so as, one and the same it cannot be.

First, a turn, wherein we look forward to God, and with our whole heart resolve to turn to Him. Then, a turn again, wherein we look backward to our sins, wherein we have turned from God: and with beholding them, our very heart breaketh. These two are two distinct, both in nature and names. One, conversion from sin; the other, contrition for sin. One, resolving to amend that which is to come; the other, reflecting and sorrowing for that which is past. One, declining from evil to be done hereafter; the other, sentencing itself for evil done heretofore. These two between them make up a complete repentance, or a perfect revolution.

Sermon Four on Repentance: Ash Wednesday 1619

A Prayer of Intercession

Remember us all, Lord, for good.
Have pity on us all, be reconciled with us all.
Fill our storehouses;
Preserve our marriages, nurture our children;
Lead forward our youth, sustain our old;
Comfort the weak-hearted, gather the scattered;
Restore the wanderers, and unite them to your Church.
Set free the troubled;
Voyage with the voyagers, travel with the travellers;
Protect the widow, shield the orphan;
Rescue the captive, heal the sick.
Remember O Lord, all those who are on trial,
In exile, or in whatever affliction,
And remember all those who need your great mercy.

Remember those who love us, and those who hate us;
Remember those who through ignorance and forgetfulness
We have not mentioned.
Pour out your rich pity and save all your people, O Lord.

A Prayer of Confession

O lover of men, O Father of mercies.
You are rich in mercy to all who call upon you.
I have sinned.
I am not fit to be called your son,
Nor to be your servant.
But I repent!
Help my impenitence and be merciful to me.
Deep calls to deep:
My deep misery calls to your deep compassion.
Where sin has abounded let grace abound more fully.
Overcome my evil with your goodness;
Let mercy rejoice against judgement.

A Prayer for Grace

I will lift up my hands to your commandments,
The commandments I have loved.
Open my eyes that I may see;
Incline my heart that I may desire;
Order my steps that I may follow
The way of your commandments.
O Lord God, be my God,
You alone, no one else, nothing else, beside you.
May I worship you and serve you
In truth of spirit, in reverence of body,
In blessing of lips.

An Evening Prayer

The day is over, and I give you thanks, O Lord.
Evening is at hand; furnish it with brightness.
Each day has its evening, and so also has life.
The evening of life is age.
Age has overtaken me; furnish it with brightness.
Do not forsake me now that my strength is failing;
But bear me, carry me, deliver me, to my old age,

To the time of my white hair.
Stay with me, Lord, for evening is coming,
And the day of this fretful life is far spent.
May your strength be made perfect in my weakness.

Private Prayers

Thomas Campion
1567–1620

*Campion, a friend of Shakespeare, Jonson and Donne, was a physician
as well as a poet and musician. He composed court masques, and his
death in 1620 was likely to have been on account of the plague.*

To Music bent is my retired mind.
   And fain would I some song of pleasure sing,
But in vain joys no comfort now I find;
   From heavenly thoughts all true delight doth spring.
Thy power, O God, thy mercies, to record,
Will sweeten every note and every word.

All earthly pomp or beauty to express
   Is but to carve in snow, on waves to write.
Celestial things, though men conceive them less,
   Yet fullest are they in themselves of light;
Such beams they yield as know no means to die,
Such heat they cast as lifts the Spirit high.

Never weather-beaten sail more willingly bent to shore,
Never tired pilgrim's limbs affected slumber more,
Than my wearied sprite now longs to fly out of my troubled
                                     breast.
O come quickly, sweetest Lord, and take my soul to rest.

Ever blooming are the joys of heaven's high paradise,
Cold age deafs not there our ears, nor vapour dims our eyes;
Glory there the sun outshines, whose beams the blessèd only
                                       see;
O come quickly, glorious Lord, and raise my sprite to thee.

John Donne
1572–1631

John Donne's calling to the priesthood came by an unusual route. At the age of 29 he secretly married the niece of his employer, Sir Thomas Egerton, Lord Keeper of the Great Seal, for which act James I considered Donne too untrustworthy for public service and advised him to enter the Church instead. His sermons are some of the best in the language and his congregations filled St Paul's Cathedral, where he was Dean.

Batter my heart, three person'd God; for, you
As yet but knocke, breathe, shine, and seeke to mend;
That I may rise, and stand, o'erthrow mee, and bend
Your force, to breake, blowe, burn and make me new.
I, like an usurpt towne, t'another due,
Labour t'admit you, but Oh, to no end,
Reason your viceroy in mee, mee should defend,
But is captiv'd, and proves weake or untrue.
Yet dearely I love you, and would be loved faine,
But am betroth'd unto your enemie;
Divorce mee, untie, or breake that knot againe,
Take mee to you, imprison mee, for I
Except you enthrall mee, never shall be free,
Nor ever chast, except you ravish mee.

Holy Sonnets XIV

From being anxious, or secure,
Dead clods of sadnesse, or light squibs of mirth,
From thinking, that great courts immure
All, or no happinesse, or that this earth
　　Is only for our prison fram'd,
　　Or that thou art covetous
To them thou lovest, or that they are maim'd
From reaching this worlds sweet, who thee seek thus,
With all thy might, Good Lord deliver us.

From needing danger, to bee good,
From owing thee yesterdaies teares to day,

From trusting so much to thy blood,
That in that hope, wee wound our soule away,
    From bribing thee with Almes to excuse
    Some sinne more burdenous,
From light affecting, in religion, newes,
From thinking us all soule, neglecting thus
Our mutual duties, Lord deliver us.

    When senses, which thy souldiers are,
Wee arme against thee, and they fight for sinne,
When want, sent but to tame, doth warre
And worke despaire a breach to enter in,
    When plenty, God's image, and seale
    Makes us Idolatrous,
And love it, not him, whom it should reveale,
When wee are mov'd to seeme religious
Only to vent wit, Lord deliver us.

– from 'The Litanie'

We would wonder, to see a man, who in a wood, were left to his liberty to fell what trees he would, take only the crooked, and leave the straightest trees; but that man, hath perchance a ship to build, and not a house, and so hath use of that kind of timber. Let not us, who know that in his [God's] house there are many mansions, but yet have no model, no design of the building, wonder at his taking in of his materials, why he takes the young, and leaves the old, or why the sickly o'erlive those that had better health.

– from a letter to Lady Kingsmile on the death of her
husband

Sir,
Every Tuesday I make account that I turn a great hourglass, and consider that a week's life is run out since I writ. But if I ask myself what I have done in the last watch, or would do in the next, I can say nothing; if I say that I have passed it without hurting any, so may the spider in my window. The primitive monks were excusable in their retirings and enclosures of themselves: for even of them every one cultivated his own garden and orchard, that is his soul and body, by

meditation, and manufactures; and they owed the world no more since they consumed none of her sweetness, nor begot others to burden her.

But for me, if I were able to husband all my time so thriftily, as not only not to wound my soul in any minute by actual sin, but not to rob and cozen her by giving any part to pleasure or business, but bestow it all upon her in meditation, yet even in that I should wound her more, and contract another guiltiness: as the eagle were very unnatural if because she is able to do it, she should perch a whole day upon a tree, staring in contemplation of the majesty and glory of the sun, and let her young eaglets starve in the nest.

Two of the most precious things which God hath afforded us here, for the agony and exercise of our sense and spirit, which are a thirst and inhiation after the next life, and a frequency of prayer and meditation in this, are often envenomed, and putrefied, and stray into corrupt disease. For as God doth thus occasion, and positively concur to evil, that when a man is purposed to do a great sin, God infuses some good thoughts which make him choose a less sin, or leave out some circumstance which aggravated that; so the devil doth not only suffer but provoke us to some things naturally good, upon condition that we shall omit some other more necessary and more obligatory.

And this is his greatest subtlety; because herein we have the deceitful comfort of having done well, and can very hardly spy our error because it is but an insensible omission, and no accusing act.

With the first of these I have often suspected myself to be overtaken; which is, with a desire of the next life: which though I know it is not merely out of a weariness of this, because I had the same desires when I went with the tide, and enjoyed fairer hopes than now: yet I doubt worldly encumbrances have increased it.

I would not that death should take me asleep. I would not have him merely seize me, and only declare me to be dead, but win me, and overcome me. When I must shipwreck, I would do it in a sea, where mine impotency might have some excuse; not in a sullen weedy lake, where I could not have so much as exercise for my swimming. Therefore I would fain do something; but that I cannot tell what, is no wonder. For to choose, is to do: but to be no part of any body, is to be nothing. At most, the greatest persons, are but great wens, and excrescences; men of wit and delightful conversation, but as moles for ornament, except they be so incorporated into the body of the world, that they contribute something to the sustentation of the whole.

– from a letter to Sir Henry Goodyere

But when we consider with a religious seriousness the manifold weaknesses of the strongest devotions in time of prayer, it is a sad consideration. I throw myself down in my chamber, and I call in and invite God and his angels thither.

And when they are there, I neglect God and his angels for the noise of a fly, for the rattling of a coach, for the whining of a door; I talk on, in the same posture of praying: eyes lifted up, knees bowed down, as though I prayed to God.

And if God or his angels should ask me, when I last thought of God in that prayer, I cannot tell. Sometimes I find that I had forgot what I was about, but when I began to forget it, I cannot tell. A memory of yesterday's pleasures, a fear of tomorrow's dangers, a straw under my knee, a noise in my ear, a light in mine eye, an anything, a nothing, a fancy, a chimera in my brain, troubles me in my prayer. So certainly there is nothing, nothing in spiritual things, perfect in this world.

– from a sermon preached at the funeral of
Sir William Cokayne

Every man is under that complicated disease, and that riddling distemper, not to be content with the most, and yet to be proud of the least thing he has; that when he looks upon men he despises them, because he is some kind of officer, and when he looks upon God, he murmurs at him, because he made him not a king.

Christmas Day sermon preached at St Pauls, 1627

William Laud
1573–1645

Archbishop Laud provoked an extraordinary degree of hatred from the Puritans when he enforced High Church uniformity on Charles I's Church. Charged with high treason by Parliament, he continued loyal to the Church of England right up to his execution.

On Religious Ceremony

No external action in the world can be uniform without some ceremonies; and these in religion, the ancienter they be the better, so they may fit time and place. Too many overburden the service of God, and too few leave it naked. And scarce anything hath hurt religion more in these broken times than an opinion in too many men, that because Rome had thrust some unnecessary and many superstitious ceremonies upon the Church, therefore the Reformation must have none at all; not considering therewhile, that ceremonies are the hedge that fence the substance of religion from all the indignities which profaneness and sacrilege too commonly put upon it. And a great weakness it is, not to see the strength which ceremonies – things weak enough in themselves, God knows – add even to religion itself.

Works, vol. II

Speech at his Execution

For myself, I am (and I acknowledge it in all humility) a most grievous sinner in many ways, by thought, word, and deed. And yet I cannot doubt that God hath mercy in store for me, a poor penitent, as well as for other sinners. I have now upon this sad occasion ransacked every corner of my heart; and yet I thank God I have not found among the many, any one sin which deserves death by any known law of this Kingdom. And yet hereby I charge nothing upon my Judges; for if they proceed upon proof by valuable witnesses, I or any other Innocent may be justly condemned. And I thank God, though the weight of the Sentence lie heavy upon me, I am as quiet within as ever I was in my life . . .

But I have done. I forgive all the world, all and every of

those bitter enemies which have persecuted me; and humbly desire to be forgiven of God first, and then of every man. And so I heartily desire you to join in prayer with me:

Lord, I am coming as fast as I can. I know that I must pass through the shadow of death, before I can come to see Thee . . . Thou by Thy Merits and Passion hast broke through the jaws of death. So, Lord, receive my soul, and have mercy upon me; and bless this Kingdom with peace and plenty, and with brotherly love and charity, that there may not be this effusion of Christian blood among them, for Jesus Christ His sake, if it be Thy will. Lord, receive my soul.

Devotions Compiled and Used by Dr William Laud

Joseph Hall
1574–1656

Joseph Hall was a moderate Puritan who suffered imprisonment and seizure of his property because he defended the episcopacy (he was bishop first of Exeter then of Norwich). His Meditations *were a Protestant substitute for the Ignatian exercises.*

That he be constant; and that, in time and matter

Those, that meditate by snatches and uncertain fits, when only all other employments forsake them, or when good motions are thrust upon them by necessity, let them never hope to reach to any perfection: for these feeble beginnings of lukewarm grace, which are wrought in them by one fit of serious meditation, are soon extinguished by intermission; and, by miswonting, perish. This day's meal, though large and liberal, strengthens thee not for to morrow: the body languisheth, if there be not a daily supply of repast. Thus feed thy soul by meditation. Set thine hours, and keep them; and yield not to an easy distraction. There is no hardness in this practice, but in the beginning: use shall give it, not ease only, but delight.

That he be constant in the continuance

What are we the warmer, if we pass hastily along by the hearth, and stay not at it? Those, that do only travel through Afric, become not blackamoors: but those, which are born there; those that inhabit there. We account those damsels too light of their love, which betroth themselves upon the first sight, upon the first motion; and those we deem of much price, which require long and earnest soliciting. He deceiveth himself, that thinketh grace so easily won: there must be much suit and importunity, ere it will yield to our desires.

Of the Place

Solitariness of Place is fittest for meditation. Retire thyself from others, if thou wouldest talk profitably with thyself. So Jesus meditates alone in the mount; Isaac, in the fields; John Baptist, in the desert; David, on his bed; Chrysostom, in the bath: each, in several places; but all solitary. There is no place free from God; none, to which he is more tied: one finds his closet most convenient; where his eyes, being limited by the known walls, call the mind, after a sort, from wandering abroad: another findeth his soul more free, when it beholdeth his heaven above and about him. It matters not, so he be solitary and silent.

Of the Time

One Time cannot be prescribed to all: for, neither is God bound to hours, neither doth the contrary disposition of men agree in one choice of opportunities. The golden hours of the morning, some find fittest for meditation; when the body, newly raised, is well calmed with his late rest; and the soul hath not as yet had, from these outward things, any motives of alienation. Others find it best, to learn wisdom of their reins in the night; hoping, with Job, that their bed will bring them comfort in their meditation; when, both all other things are still; and themselves, wearied with these earthly cares, do, out of a contempt of them, grow into greater liking and love of heavenly things. I have ever found Isaac's time fittest, who went out in the evening, to meditate. No precept, no practice of others can prescribe to us, in this circumstance. It shall be enough, that, first, we set ourselves a time:

secondly, that we set apart that time, wherein we are aptest for this service.

A Taste and Relish of what we have thought upon

In meditation we do both see and Taste; but we see, before we taste: sight, is of the understanding; taste, of the affection: neither can we see, but we must taste; we cannot know aright, but we must needs be affected. Let the heart, therefore, first conceive and feel in itself the sweetness or bitterness of the matter meditated: which is never done, without some passion; nor expressed, without some hearty exclamation.

The Art of Divine Meditation

Augustine Baker
1575–1641

A convert to Roman Catholicism, Baker became a monk in the English Benedictine Congregation, and gained a high reputation as a spiritual counsellor. His teaching was closely based on that of Walter Hilton, and continued a source of teaching for generations of English Catholics.

Duties of Novices

Daily experience confirms that which spiritual writers observe, that God in great goodness to souls does usually upon their first conversion bestow upon them a great fervour in divine and religious duties. Good souls, therefore, are often to be exhorted to make good use of this fervour, and to improve it diligently (yet with discretion), thereby to produce in their hearts an unshaken resolution to proceed in the ways of the divine love, notwithstanding any contradiction or pain that may happen. They must not expect this fervour will be lasting.

Of Scrupulosity

Now concerning temptations in general, the devout soul is to consider that it is no sin to have them; yea, being sent us by God, they are meant for our good, and to give us occasion to merit by them. And those which God sends us are the most proper for us; for if they were in our own choice we should choose least and last of all those that are most fit to humble us, and to withdraw our affections from ourselves and creatures; so that the more displeasing to us and afflicting that any temptations are the more profitable are they.

Certain it is that however troublesome and horrid soever such temptations may seem to be, yet they, being quietly resisted, or rather neglected, do wonderfully purify the soul, establishing Divine love most firmly and deeply in the spirit. Moreover, by occasion of them the superior soul is enabled to transcend all the disorders and tumults in inferior nature, adhering to God during the greatest contradictions of sensuality.

Of Sensible Devotion

In case that internal distresses in prayer be so violent, that the soul, to her seeming, can only keep herself in an outward posture of prayer; all that she thinks or does appearing to her so utterly void of all spirit of devotion, love, and reverence to God that she may rather suspect it to be injurious to Him; let her be patient and abstain from disquieting her mind with murmering complaints, and by all means let her be sure not to betake herself to consolation in creatures or recreative diversions in times appointed for recollection, and then all will be very well.

Holy Wisdom

John Selden
1584–1654

John Selden is now remembered mainly for his Table Talk, *snippets of his conversation recorded by his secretary. In his time, though, he was a considerable jurist and parliamentarian and would have been a formidable one had he not held his tongue when he disagreed with his colleagues.*

Prayer should be short, without giving God Almighty reasons why he should grant this or that; he knows best what is good for us. If your boy should ask you a suit of clothes, and give you reasons, 'otherwise he cannot wait upon you, he cannot go abroad but he will discredit you,' would you endure it? You know it better than he; let him ask a suit of clothes.

If a servant that has been fed with good beef, goes into that part of England where salmon is plenty, at first he is pleased with his salmon, and despises his beef, but after he has been there a while, he grows weary of his salmon, and wishes for his good beef again. We have a while been much taken with this praying by the spirit; but in time we may grow weary of it, and wish for our Common Prayer.

Religion is like the fashion: one man wears his doublet slashed, another laced, another plain; but every man has a doublet. So every man has his religion. We differ about trimming.

Men say they are of the same religion for quietness sake; but if the matter were well examined you would scarce find three anywhere of the same religion in all points.

Table Talk

Mary Ward
1585–1645

Mary Ward, a Roman Catholic from Yorkshire, founded the Institute of the Blessed Virgin Mary, a religious order for women based on the life of the Jesuits. She was fiercely opposed both for her Catholic faith, and for her assertion of the spiritual equality of men and women. The Institute subsequently spread across the world.

Now, sisters, since God has particularly looked upon you, calling you to this state of life and giving you this vocation, I doubt not but that some of you thirst greatly after the effecting of his will, and so have patience when you find yourselves profited no more. Now you are to understand how you are to attain to this perfection. By learning? No, though learning be a good means, because it giveth knowledge. Yet you see many learned men who are not perfect because they practise not what they know, nor perform what they preach. But to attain perfection, knowledge of verity is necessary, to love it and to effect it. That you may not err, I beseech you all to understand and note well wherefore you are to seek this knowledge. Not for the content and satisfaction it bringeth, though it be exceeding great, but for the end it bringeth you to, which is God. Seek it for him, who is Verity. Then you will be happy and able to profit yourselves and others. Without it you shall never be fit for anything.

This is verity: to do what we have to do well. Many think it nothing to do ordinary things. But for us it is. To do ordinary things well, to keep our Constitutions, and all other things that be ordinary in every office or employment whatsoever it be. To do it well: this is for us, and this by God's grace will maintain fervour.

There was a Father that came recently to England, whom I heard say that he would not for a thousand worlds be a woman, because he thought that a woman could not apprehend God! I answered nothing but only smiled, although I could have answered him by the experience I have of the contrary.

The other day, disputing with a Father who loves you well, I could not make him think otherwise than that women are yet by nature full of fears and affections, more than men, which, with respect to him, is not so. It is true if we will not place our knowledge right, we shall be full of fears and affections. We shall fear that which is not to be feared and, remaining in troubles, love and adhere to that which is not worthy of love. We know that God only is to be feared and he only is worthy of love. Remember then that he be the end of all your actions and therein you will find great satisfaction and think all things easy and possible.

Till God Will

If thou feelest in thy self a desire to perform a virtuous work very profitable to the great honour of God, but hast no opportunity of fulfilling it, rejoice if others bring it to pass instead of thee; for if God is served, what does it matter from whom He receive the service?

Whatever falls to thee to do, that perform as much as thou canst faithfully and diligently; but be not too anxious as to how it may turn out, nor whether it will be hazardous or not, but commit it to the good God.

The Spirit of Mary Ward

Robert Herrick
1591–1674

A priest and a poet, Robert Herrick lost the living of Dean Prior, near Totnes in Devonshire, during the Civil War, but by all accounts he enjoyed a cheerful exile in London until his own personal restoration to his parish in 1662. Here are two of the poems he wrote which were consistent with his cloth.

A Thanksgiving to God, for his House

Lord, Thou hast given me a cell
    Wherein to dwell:
A little house, whose humble roof
    Is weather-proof;
Under the sparres of which I lie
    Both soft, and drie;
Where Thou my chamber for to ward
    Hast set a guard
Of harmlesse thoughts, to watch and keep
    Me, while I sleep.
Low is my porch, as is my fate,
    Both void of state;
And yet the threshold of my doore
    Is worn by th' poor,
Who thither come, and freely get
    Good words, or meat;
Like as my parlour, so my hall
    And kitchin's small;
A little butterie, and therein
    A little byn,

Which keeps my little loafe of bread
    Unchipt, unflead;[1]
Some brittle sticks of thorne or briar
    Make me a fire,
Close by whose living coale I sit,
    And glow like it.
Lord, I confesse too, when I dine,
    The pulse is Thine,
And all those other bits, that bee
    There plac'd by Thee;
The worts, the purslain,[2] and the messe
    Of water-cresse,
Which of Thy kindnesse Thou hast sent;
    And my content
Makes those, and my beloved beet,
    To be more sweet.
'Tis thou that crown'st my glittering hearth
    With guiltless mirth;
And giv'st me wassaile bowles to drink,
    Spic'd to the brink.
Lord, 'tis Thy plenty-dropping hand,
    That soiles my land;
And giv'st me, for my bushell sowne,
    Twice ten for one:
Thou mak'st my teeming hen to lay
    Her egg each day;
Besides my healthfull ewes to beare
    Me twins each yeare;
The while the conduits of my kine
    Run creame, for wine.
All these, and better Thou dost send
    Me, to this end,
That I should render, for my part
    A thankfull heart;
Which, fir'd with incense, I resigne,
    As wholly Thine;
But the acceptance, that must be,
    My Christ, by Thee.

1 i.e. uncontaminated   2 a salad vegetable

His Confession

Look how our foule dayes do exceed our faire;
And as our bad, more then our good works are,
Ev'n so those lines, pen'd by my wanton wit,
Treble the number of these good I've writ.
Things precious are least num'rous; men are prone
To do ten bad, for one good action.

Nicholas Ferrar
1592–1637

Giving up a promising career in business and politics, Nicholas Ferrar founded the Little Gidding Community in 1626. The Community contained both families and single people, bound together by a common rule of prayer and service. The following words were spoken by Nicholas before his death, as he handed over the leadership of the Community to his brother John.

My dear brother, I am now shortly to appear before my good Lord God, to whom I must give account of what I have said and taught you all of this family in the ways and service of God. I have, I tell you, delivered unto you nothing but what is agreeable to His holy will, law and word, how you should love Him, serve Him, and have showed you the right and good way that leadeth to life everlasting; what you ought to believe, what to do and practise, according to those abilities God shall give each of you, and places He shall call you unto. It is the right, good, old way you are in; keep in it. God will be worshipped in spirit and truth, in body and in soul, He will have both inward love and fear, and outward reverence of body and gesture. You, I say, know the way; keep in it: I will not use more words, you have lessons enow given you; be constant to them. I now tell you, that you may be fore-warned and prepare for it, there will be sad times come, and very sad. You will live to see them, but be courageous and hold you fast to God with humility and patience, rely upon His mercy and power. You will suffer much, but God will help you; and you will be sifted, and endeavour will be made to turn you out of the right way, the good way you are in, even by those whom you least think of, and your troubles will be many. But be you steadfast and call upon God, and He in His good and due time will help you. Keep on your daily prayers and let all be done in sincerity, setting God always before your eyes.

The Life of Nicholas Ferrar

George Herbert
1593–1633

George Herbert is one of England's foremost Christian poets. After a successful academic career at Cambridge, he was ordained in 1626. He first had the living at Leighton Bromswold, near his friend Nicholas Ferrar's community at Little Gidding, and he refurbished Leighton church according to his ideal of how worship should be conducted. In 1630 he went to Bemerton, near Salisbury, where he wrote The Country Parson, *a description of the pattern of ministry to which he aspired.*

The Parson a Master of Himself

The Country Parson is exceedingly exact in his life, being holy, just, prudent, temperate, bold, grave, in all his ways. And because the two highest points of life, wherein a Christian is most seen, are patience and mortification; patience in regard of afflictions, moritification in regard of lusts and affections, and the stupefying and deading of all the clamorous powers of the soul, therefore he hath thoroughly studied these, that he may be an absolute master and commander of himself, for all the purposes which God hath ordained him.

The Parson's Library

The Country Parson's library is a holy life . . . He that hath considered how to carry himself at table about his appetite, if he tell this to another, preacheth; and much more feelingly, and judiciously, than he writes his rules of temperance out of books. So that the parson having studied and mastered all his lusts and affections within, and the whole army of temptations without, hath ever so many sermons ready penned, as he hath victories.

His Diverse Knowledge

The Country Parson is full of all knowledge . . . He conde-
scends even to the knowledge of tillage, and pasturage, and
makes great use of them in teaching, because people, by what
they understand, are best led to what they understand not.

God's Hand in all Things

The Country Parson considering the great aptness country
people have, to think that all things come by a kind of natural
course; and that if they sow and soil their grounds, they must
have corn; if they keep and fodder well their cattle, they must
have milk, and calves; labours to reduce them to see God's
hand in all things, and to believe that things are not set in
such an inevitable order, but that God often changeth it
according as he sees fit, either for reward or punishment. To
this end he represents to his flock, that God hath, and exer-
ciseth a threefold power in every thing which concerns man.
The first is a sustaining power; the second, a governing power;
the third, a spiritual power.

By his sustaining power he preserves and actuates every
thing in his being; so that corn doth not grow by any other
virtue, than by that which he continually supplies, as the
corn needs it; without which supply the corn would instantly
dry up, as a river would, if the fountain were stopped . . .

By God's governing power he preserves and orders the
references of things one to the other, so that though the corn
do grow, and be preserved in that act by his sustaining power,
yet if he suit not other things to the growth, as seasons, and
weather, and other accidents, by his governing power, the
fairest harvests come to nothing. And it is observable, that
God delights to have men feel, and acknowledge, and reverence his power, and therefore he often overturns things, when
they are thought past danger . . . Now this he doth, that men
should perpetuate, and not break off their acts of dependence,
how fair soever the opportunities present themselves . . .

The third power is spiritual, by which God turns all
outward blessings to inward advantages. So that if a farmer
hath both a fair harvest, and that also well inned, and
imbarned, and continuing safe there; yet if God give him not
the grace to use and utter this well, all his advantages are to

his loss. And it is observable in this, how God's goodness strives with man's refractoriness; man would sit down at this world, God bids him sell it, and purchase a better.

The Country Parson

Deniall

When my devotions could not pierce
Thy silent eares;
Then was my heart broken, as was my verse:
My breast was full of fears
And disorder:

My bent thoughts, like a brittle bow,
Did flie asunder:
Each took his way; some would to pleasures go,
Some to the warres and thunder
Of alarms.

As good go any where, they say,
As to benumme
Both knees and heart, in crying night and day,
Come, come, my God, O come,
But no hearing.

O that thou shouldst give dust a tongue
To crie to thee,
And then not heare it crying! all day long
My heart was in my knee,
But no hearing.

Therefore my soul lay out of sight,
Untun'd, unstrung:
My feeble spirit, unable to look right,
Like a nipt blossome, hung
Discontented.

O cheer and tune my heartlesse breast,
Deferre no time;
That so thy favours granting my request,
They and my minde may chime,
And mend my ryme.

Bitter-sweet

Ah my deare angrie Lord,
Since thou dost love, yet strike;
Cast down, yet help afford;
Sure I will do the like.

I will complain, yet praise;
I will bewail, approve:
And all my sowre-sweet dayes
I will lament, and love.

Love

Love bade me welcome; yet my soul drew back,
    Guiltie of dust and sinne.
But quick-ey'd Love, observing me grow slack
    From my first entrance in,
Drew nearer to me, sweetly questioning,
    If I lack'd any thing.

A guest, I answer'd, worthy to be here:
    Love said, You shall be he.
I the unkinde, ungratefull? Ah my deare,
    I cannot look on thee.
Love took my hand, and smiling did reply,
    Who made the eyes but I?

Truth Lord, but I have marr'd them: let my shame
    Go where it doth deserve.
And know you not, sayes Love, who bore the blame?
    My deare, then I will serve.
You must sit down, sayes Love, and taste my meat:
    So I did sit and eat.

Izaak Walton
1593–1683

Walton was an ironmonger who would leave his shop in London to go fishing and who enjoyed forty years in retirement. He produced a peculiarly English version of saints' lives – gently admiring biographies of near contemporaries like Herbert, Donne and Hooker – some of which were based on fact.

George Herbert

His chiefest recreation was music, in which heavenly art he was a most excellent master, and composed many divine hymns and anthems, which he set and sung to his lute or viol; and though he was a lover of retiredness, yet his love of music was such, that he went usually twice every week, on certain appointed days, to the cathedral church in Salisbury; and at his return would say, That his time spent in prayer, and cathedral music, elevated his soul, and was his Heaven upon Earth. But before his return thence to Bemerton, he would usually sing and play his part at an appointed private music meeting; and, to justify this practice, he would often say, Religion does not banish mirth, but only moderates and sets rules to it.

And, as his desire to enjoy his Heaven upon Earth drew him twice every week to Salisbury, so, his walks thither were the occasion of many accidents to others . . .

In one of his walks . . . he saw a poor man with a poorer horse, that was fallen under his load; they were both in distress and needed present help; which Mr Herbert percciving, put off his canonical coat, and helped the poor man to unload, and after to load his horse. The poor man blessed him for it, and he blessed the poor man; and was so like the good Samaritan, that he gave him money to refresh both himself and his horse; and told him: That if he loved himself, he should be merciful to his beast.

Thus he left the poor man; and at his coming to his musical friends at Salisbury, they began to wonder that Mr George Herbert, which used to be so trim and clean, came into that company so soiled and discomposed; but he told then the occasion. And when one of the company told him: He had disparaged himself by so dirty an employment, his answer was: That the thought of what he had done, would prove music to him at midnight; and that the omission of it would have upbraided and made discord in his conscience, whensoever he should pass by that place; for if I be bound to pray for all that be in distress, I am sure that I am bound, so far as it is in my power, to practise what I pray for. And though I do not wish for the like occasion every day, yet let me tell you, I would not willingly pass one day of my life, without comforting a sad soul, or showing mercy; and I praise God for this occasion. And now let us tune our instruments.

The Life of George Herbert

Sir Thomas Browne
1605–1682

Browne, a Norfolk physician, belonged to one of the first generations to be born and brought up a Protestant and was therefore much more relaxed about it than his convert forebears. In his immensely popular Religio Medici *('the religion of a doctor'), he discusses his religious views – and anything else that takes his fancy.*

Of Religious Civility

I am, I confess, naturally inclined to that which misguided zeal terms superstition; my common conversation I do acknowledge austere, my behaviour full of rigour, sometimes not without morosity; yet at my devotion I love to use the civility of my knee, my hat, and hand, with all those outward and sensible motions which may express or promote my invisible devotion. I should violate my own arm rather than a Church, nor willingly deface the memory of Saint or Martyr. At the sight of a Cross or Crucifix I can dispense with my hat, but scarce with the thought or memory of my Saviour; I cannot laugh at but rather pity the fruitless journeys of Pilgrims, or contemn the miserable condition of Friars; for though misplaced in circumstance, there is something in it of devotion: I could never hear the *Ave Marie* Bell without an elevation, or think it a sufficient warrant, because they erred in one circumstance, for me to err in all, that is in silence and dumb contempt.

Religio Medici

Thomas Washbourne
1606–1687

Washbourne's occasional poem means that this anthology can include at least one piece about the vagaries of the English weather. The poem also happens to be a good one – despite the obscurity of its author – touching on Parliament's temporary abolition of Christmas and bringing this round to a note of personal repentance.

Upon a Great Shower of Snow that Fell on May-Day, 1654

You that are weather-wise and pretend to know
Long time before, when it will rain or snow,
When 'twill be fair or foul, when hot or cold –
Here stand or gaze a while, I dare be bold
To say you never saw the like; nay more,
You never heard the like of this before.
Since snow in May, you may hereafter make
A famous epoch in your almanac.
Prodigious 'tis, and I begin to fear
We have mistook the season of the year;
'Tis Winter yet, and this is Christmas day,
Which we indeed miscall the first of May.
Summer and Winter now confounded be,
And we no difference betwixt them see,
Only the trees are blossomed, and so
The Glastonbury hawthorn used to do,
Upon the day of Christ's nativity,
As Camden tells in his Chorography.
The youths for cold creep in the chimney's end,
Who formerly the day did spritely spend
In merry May-games; now they hang the head
And droop, as if they and their sports were dead.
Perhaps some superstitious Cavalier,

That loved to keep his Christmas, will go near
To make an ill interpretation
Of this, and call it a judgement on the Nation
For our despising of that time and season
Against the ancient custom and right reason,
As he conceives, and since we'll not allow
One in December, we have a Christmas now.
But we a better use may make of it;
Though not to our minds the weather fit,
Yet to our soul convert the same, and thence
Extract this wholesome holy inference:
From this unseasonable change of weather
Without us, what's within us we may gather;
When in our hearts the Summer should begin
And graces grow, 'tis Winter by one sin,
All frost and snow, nothing comes up that's good,
And fruits o' th' Spirit nipped are in the bud.
Our May's turned to December, and our sun
Declines before he half his course hath run.
O Thou the Sun of Righteousness! display
Thy beams of mercy, make it once more May
Within our souls; let it shine warm and clear,
Producing in us yet a fruitful year.
Let it dissolve our snow into a shower
Of hot and penitent tears, which may procure
A blessing on the Nation, and at last
A general pardon for all faults are past.

John Milton
1608–1674

Before composing Paradise Lost *in his fifties Milton spent many years writing pamphlets in defence of the English Commonwealth, some of which display rather less sublimity than his major work. These two pieces come from that period, the sonnet referring to his approaching blindness.*

Sonnet

When I consider how my light is spent,
    Ere half my days, in this dark world and wide,
    And that one talent which is death to hide
    Lodged with me useless, though my soul more bent
To serve therewith my Maker, and present
    My true account, lest he returning chide,
    'Doth God exact day-labour, light denied?'
    I fondly ask. But Patience, to prevent
That murmur, soon replies: 'God doth not need
    Either man's work or his own gifts; who best
    Bear his mild yoke, they serve him best. His state
Is kingly; thousands at his bidding speed
    And post o'er land and ocean without rest;
    They also serve who only stand and wait.'

Against Fugitive and Cloistered Virtue

Good and evil we know in the field of this World grow up together almost inseparably; and the knowledge of good is so involved and interwoven with the knowledge of evil and in so many cunning resemblances hardly to be discerned, that those confused seeds which were imposed on *Psyche* as an incessant labour to cull out and sort asunder were not more intermixed. It was from out the rind of one apple tasted that the knowledge of good and evil as two twins cleaving together leapt forth into the World. And perhaps this is that doom which *Adam* fell into of knowing good and evil, that is to say of knowing good by evil. As therefore the state of man now is, what wisdom can there be to choose, what continence to forbeare, without the knowledge of evil? He that can apprehend and consider vice with all her baits and seeming pleasures, and yet abstain, and yet distinguish, and yet prefer that which is truly better, he is the true warfaring Christian. I cannot praise a fugitive and cloistered virtue, unexercised and unbreathed, that never sallies out and sees her adversary, but slinks out of the race, where that immortal garland is to be run for not without dust and heat. Assuredly we bring not innocence into the world, we bring impurity much rather: that which purifies us is trial, and trial is by what is contrary.

Areopagitica

Jeremy Taylor
1613–1667

Englishmen admire Hooker, but they love Taylor, remarked Dr Palmer, the Whig theologian, referring to the gentleness and courtesy which eased Taylor's position as a High Churchman during the Civil War. Nevertheless, he was imprisoned four times by the Parliamentarians, but upon the Restoration became Bishop of Down and Connor. His devotional writings are filled with practical advice and psychological insight.

The more we love, the better we are; and the greater our friendships are, the dearer we are to God. Let them be as dear, and let them be as perfect, and let them be as many, as you can; there is no danger in it; only where the restraint begins, there begins our imperfection . . . As all our graces here are but imperfect, that is, at the best they are but tendencies to glory; so our friendships are imperfect too, and but beginnings of a celestial friendship, by which we shall love every one as much as they can be loved . . .

The universal friendship of which I speak, must be limited, because we are so: in those things where we stand next to immensity and infinity, as in good wishes and prayers, and a readiness to benefit all mankind, in these our friendships must not be limited: but in other things which pass under our hand and eye, our voices and our material exchanges; our hands can reach no further but to our arms' end, and our voices can but sound till the next air be quiet.

Friendship

Care of our Time

We must remember that the life of every man may be so ordered, and indeed must, that it may be a perpetual serving of God. For God provides the good things of the world to serve the needs of nature by the labours of the ploughman, the skill and pains of the artisan, and the dangers and traffic of the merchant: these men are, in their calling, the ministers of the Divine Providence, and the stewards of the creation, and servants of a great family of God, the world, in the employment of procuring necessaries for food and clothing, ornament and physic. In their proportions also a king and a priest and a prophet, a judge and an advocate, doing the works of their employment according to their proper rules, are doing the work of God. So that no man can complain that his calling takes him off from religion; his calling itself, and his employment in honest trades and offices is a serving of God; and if it be moderately pursued, and according to the rules of Christian prudence, will leave void spaces enough for prayers and retirements of a more spiritual religion.

Contentedness in all Estates and Accidents

God is the master of the scenes; we must not choose which part we shall act; it concerns us only to be careful that we do it well, always saying, 'If this please God, let it be as it is . . .'

For is not all the world God's family? Are not we His creatures? Do we not live upon His meat, and move by His strength, and do our work by His light? And shall there be a mutiny among the flocks and herds, because their lord or their shepherd chooses their pastures, and suffers them not to wander into deserts and unknown ways? If we choose, we do it so foolishly that we cannot like it long, and most commonly not at all; but God is wise, affectionate to our needs, and powerful. Here, therefore, is the wisdom of the contented man, to let God choose for him; for when we have given up our wills to Him, our spirits must needs rest, while our conditions have for their security the power, the wisdom, and the charity of God . . .

Let us prepare our minds against changes, always expecting them, that we be not surprised when they come;

for nothing is so great an enemy to tranquility and a contented spirit as unreadiness when our fortunes are violently changed. Our spirits are unchanged if they always stood in the suburbs and expectation of sorrows.

Holy Living

He that would die well, must all the days of his life lay up against the day of death . . . But this is to be the work of our life, and not to be done at once; but, as God gives us time, by succession, by parts and little periods.

The Fear of Death

Of all the evils of the world which are reproached with an evil character, Death is the most innocent of its accusation. For when it is present, it hurts nobody; and when it is absent, it is indeed troublesome, but the trouble is owing to our fears, not to the affrighting and mistaken object: and besides this, if it were an evil, it is so transient, that it passes like the instant or undiscerned portion of the present time; and either it is past, or it is not yet; for just when it is, no man hath reason to complain of so insensible, so sudden, so undiscerned a change.

It is so harmless a thing, that no good man was ever thought the more miserable for dying, but much the happier.

Justice in Sickness

Every man will forgive a dying person; and therefore let the sick man be ready and sure, if he can, to send to such persons whom he hath injured, and beg their pardon, and do them right: For in this case he cannot stay for an opportunity of convenient and advantageous reconcilement; he cannot then spin out a treaty, nor beat down the price of composition, nor lay a snare to be quit from the obligation and coercion of laws; but he must ask forgiveness downright, and make him amends as he can.

Holy Dying

Richard Crashaw
1612/13–1649

Crashaw's religious and secular poetry displays a very un-English extravagance and he ended up a disillusioned Roman Catholic in exile on the Continent. Before the Civil War forced him abroad, however, he made friends with Nicholas Ferrar and often stayed at Little Gidding, which he described in verse (see below). He was briefly vicar of Little St Mary's in Cambridge where he introduced Ferrar's practice of nightly vigils.

from 'Description of a Religious House and Condition of Life'

... Our lodgings hard and homely as our fare,
That chaste and cheap, as the few clothes we wear;
Those, coarse and negligent, as the natural locks
Of these loose groves; rough as th' unpolish'd rocks.
A hasty portion of prescribèd sleep;
Obedient slumbers, that can wake and weep,
And sing, and sigh, and work, and sleep again;
Still rolling a round sphere of still-returning pain.
Hands full of hearty labours; pains that pay
And prize themselves; do much, that more they may,
And work for work, not wages; let to-morrow's
New drops wash off the sweat of this day's sorrows.
A long and daily-dying life, which breathes
A respiration of reviving deaths.
But neither are there those ignoble stings
That nip the blossom of the World's best things,
And lash Earth-labouring souls.
No cruel guard of diligent cares, that keep
Crown'd woes awake, as things too wise for sleep:
But reverent discipline, and religious fear,
And soft obedience, find sweet biding here;
Silence, and sacred rest; peace, and pure joys;
Kind loves keep house, lie close, and make no noise;
And room enough for monarchs, while none swells
Beyond the kingdoms of contentful cells.

The self-rememb'ring soul sweetly recovers
Her kindred with the stars; not basely hovers
Below: but meditates her immortal way
Home to the original source of Light and intellectual day.

Antiphons from *'The Office of the Holy Cross'*

All hail, fair tree
Whose fruit we be!
What song shall raise
Thy seemly praise,
Who brought'st to light
Life out of death, Day out of Night!

Christ when He died
Deceived the Cross;
And on Death's side
Threw all the loss.
The captive World awaked and found
The prisoner loose, the jailor bound.

Henry More
1614–1687

For one of the Cambridge Platonists, who preferred a rational to a mystical Christianity, More showed a remarkable interest in mysticism, witchcraft and the occult. Here, though, he is arguing that spiritual problems like the existence of suffering, will be understood, if not immediately.

The affairs of this world are like a curious, but intricately contrived comedy; and we cannot judge of the tendency of what is past, or acting at present, before the entrance of the last Act, which shall bring in Righteousness in triumph; who, though she hath abided many a brunt, and has been very cruelly and despitefully used hitherto in the world, yet at last, according to our desires, we shall see the Knight overcome the Giant. For what is the reason we are so much pleased with the reading Romances and the Fictions of the Poets, but that here, as Aristotle says, things are set down as they should be; but in the true history hitherto of the world, things are recorded indeed as they are, but it is but a testimony, that they have not been as they should be? Wherefore, in the upshot of all, when we shall see that come to pass that so mightily pleases us in the reading the most ingenious plays and heroic poems, that long afflicted Virtue at last comes to the crown, the mouth of all unbelievers must be for ever stopped. And for my own part, I doubt not but that it shall so come to pass in the close of the world. But impatiently to call for vengeance upon every enormity before that time, is rudely to overturn the stage before the entrance into the fifth Act, out of ignorance of the plot of the comedy; and to prevent the solemnity of the general judgement by more paltry and particular executions.

Divine Dialogues

Richard Baxter
1615–1691

Richard Baxter was a moderate Puritan at a time when such a position won few friends. During the Commonwealth he quarrelled with Cromwell; with the Restoration he was forced out of the Church of England by the 1662 Act of Uniformity. Then, at the age of 70, he was imprisoned by Judge Jeffreys for supposed sedition. Nevertheless, throughout all this he was a powerful preacher and a beloved pastor.

Though my conscience would trouble me when I sinned, yet diverse sins I was addicted to, and oft committed against my conscience; which, for the warning of others I will confess here to my shame:

1. I was much addicted, when I feared correction, to lie, that I might 'scape.

2. I was much addicted to the excessive gluttonous eating of apples and pears; which I think laid the foundation of that imbecility and flatulency of my stomach which caused the bodily calamities of my life.

3. To this end, and to concur with naughty boys that gloried in evil, I have oft gone into other men's orchards and stolen their fruit, when I had enough at home.

4. I was somewhat excessively addicted to play, and that with covetousness, for money.

5. I was extremely bewitched with a love of romances, fables and old tales, which corrupted my affections and lost my time.

6. I was guilty of much idle foolish chat, and imitation of boys in scurrilous foolish words and actions (though I durst not swear).

7. I was too proud of my masters' commendations for learning, who all of them fed my pride, making me seven or eight years the highest in the school, and boasting of me to others, which, though it furthered my learning, yet helped not my humility.

8. I was too bold and unreverent towards my parents.

These were my sins, which, in my childhood, conscience troubled me with for a great while before they were overcome.

Many a time have I been brought very low and received the sentence of death in myself, when my poor, honest, praying neighbours have met, and upon their fasting and earnest prayers I have been recovered . . .

[One] time, having read in Dr Gerhard the admirable effects of the swallowing of a gold bullet upon his own father in a case like mine, I got a gold bullet and swallowed it (between twenty and thirty shillings' weight); and having taken it, I knew not how to be delivered of it again. I took clysters and purges for about three weeks, but nothing stirred it . . . But at last my neighbours set a day apart to fast and pray for me, and I was freed from my danger in the beginning of that day . . .

Another time, as I sat in my study, the weight of my greatest folio books broke down three or four of the highest shelves, when I sat close under them, and they fell down on every side of me, and not one of them hit me save one upon the arm; whereas the place, the weight and greatness of the books was such, and my head just under them, that it was a wonder they had not beaten out my brains . . .

All this I mention as obliged to record the mercies of my great Preserver to his praise and glory.

In my youth I was quickly past my fundamentals and was running up into a multitude of controversies, and greatly delighted with metaphysical and scholastic writings (though I must needs say my preaching was still on the necessary points). But the elder I grew the smaller stress I laid upon these controversies and curiosities (though still my intellect abhorreth confusion), as finding far greater uncertainties in them than I at first discerned and finding less usefulness comparatively, even where there is the greatest certainty. And now it is the fundamental doctrines of the Catechism which I highliest value and daily think of, and find most useful to myself and others. The Creed, the Lord's Prayer and the Ten Commandments do find me now the most acceptable and plentiful matter for all my meditations. They are to me as my daily bread and drink. And as I can speak and write of them over and over again, so I had rather read or hear of them than of any of the school niceties which once so much pleased me.

It is a marvellous great help to my faith to find it built on so sure foundations and so consonant to the law of nature. I am not so foolish as to pretend my certainty to be greater than it is merely because it is a dishonour to be less certain, nor will I by shame be kept from confessing those infirmities which those have as much as I who hypocritically reproach me with them. My certainty that I am a man is before my certainty that there is a God, for *Quod facit notum est magis notum*: my certainty that there is a God is greater than my certainty that he requireth love and holiness of his creature; my certainty of *this* is greater than my certainty of the life of reward and punishment hereafter; my certainty of that is greater than my certainty of the endless duration of it and of the immortality of individuate souls; my certainty of the Deity is greater than my certainty of the Christian Faith; my certainty of the Christian Faith in its essentials is greater than my certainty of the perfection and infallibility of all the Holy Scriptures; my certainty of that is greater than my certainty of the meaning of many particular texts, and so of the truth of certain books. So that you can see by what gradations my understanding doth proceed, so also that my certainty differeth as the evidences differ.

And they that have attained to greater perfection and a higher degree of certainty than I should pity me and produce their evidence to help me. And they that will begin all their certainty with that of the truth of the Scripture as the *principium cognoscendi* may meet me at the same end; but they must give me leave to undertake to prove to a heathen or infidel the Being of a God, and the necessity of holiness, and the certainty of a reward or a punishment, even while he yet denieth the truth of Scripture and in order to his believing it to be true.

In my younger years my trouble for sin was most about my actual failings in thought, word or action (except hardness of heart, of which more anon); but now I am much more troubled for inward defects and omission or want of the vital duties or graces of the soul. My daily trouble is so much for my ignorance of God and weakness of belief, and want of greater love to God and strangeness to him and to the life to come, and for want of a greater willingness to die, and longing to be with God in heaven, as that I take not some immoralities, though very great, to be in themselves so great and odious sins if they could be found as separate from these. Had I all the riches of the world, how gladly should I give them for a fuller knowledge, belief and love of God and everlasting glory! These wants are the greatest burden of my life, which oft maketh my life itself a burden. And I cannot find any hope of reaching so high in these while I am in the flesh as I once hoped before this time to have attained, which is honoured with so little of the knowledge of God.

I more than ever lament the unhappiness of the nobility, gentry and great ones of the world, who live in such temptation to sensuality, curiosity and wasting of their time about a multitude of little things, and whose lives are too often the transcript of the sins of Sodom, pride, fullness of bread, and abundance of idleness and want of compassion to the poor. And I more value the life of the poor labouring man, but especially of him that hath neither poverty nor riches.

The Reliquiae Baxterianae

Andrew Marvell
1621–1678

A protegé of Milton, Marvell was a poet, satirist and, briefly, MP for Hull under Richard Cromwell. He resisted being drawn into the courtly excesses of Charles II and voiced his criticism in an anonymous pamphlet against 'The Growth of Papacy and Arbitrary Government', upon which a reward was offered for the discovery of its author.

The Coronet

When for the Thorns with which I long, too long,
    With many a piercing wound
    My Saviour's head have crown'd,
I seek with Garlands to redress that Wrong,
    Through every Garden, every Mead
I gather flow'rs (my fruits are only flow'rs)
    Dismantling all the fragrant Towers
That once adorn'd my Shepherdess's head.
And now when I have summ'd up all my store,
    Thinking (so I my self deceive)
    So rich a Chaplet thence to weave
As never yet the King of Glory wore,
    Alas I find the Serpent old
    That, twining in his speckled breast,
    About the flow'rs disguis'd does fold,
    With wreaths of Fame and Interest.
Ah, foolish Man, that would'st debase with them
And mortal Glory, Heaven's Diadem!
But Thou who only could'st the Serpent tame,
Either his slipp'ry knots at once untie,
And disintangle all his winding Snare;
Or shatter too with him my curious frame
And let these wither, so that he may die,
Though set with Skill and chosen out with Care;
That they, while Thou on both their Spoils dost tread,
May crown thy Feet, that could not crown thy Head.

George Fox
1624–1691

*George Fox had that rare combination of zeal and organisational talent
which turned him from a mere reformer into a religious revolutionary,
founding the Society of Friends – the 'Quakers' – in 1652. He was
subject to visions throughout his life as an itinerant preacher and
organiser and he counselled fellow Quakers to be led by the 'inner light
of Christ' rather than the current Church dogma.*

About the beginning of the year 1647, I was moved of the
Lord to go into Derbyshire, where I met with some friendly
people, and had many discourses with them. Then passing
further into the Peak country, I met with more friendly
people, and with some in empty, high notions. And travelling
on through some parts of Leicestershire and into Nottingham-
shire, there I met with a tender people, and a very tender
woman whose name was Elizabeth Hooton; and with these I
had some meetings and discourses. But my troubles
continued, and I was often under great temptations; and I
fasted much, and walked abroad in solitary places many days,
and often took my Bible and went and sat in hollow trees
and lonesome places till night came on; and frequently in the
night walked mournfully about by myself, for I was a man of
sorrows in the times of the first workings of the Lord in me
. . .

As I cannot declare the misery I was in, it was so great
and heavy upon me, so neither can I set forth the mercies of
God unto me in all my misery. Oh, the everlasting love of
God to my soul when I was in great distress! When my
troubles and torments were great, then was his love exceeding
great. Thou, Lord, makest a fruitful field a barren wilderness,
and a barren wilderness a fruitful field; thou bringest down
and settest up; thou killest and makest alive; all honour and
glory be to thee, O Lord of glory! . . .

And when all my hopes in all men were gone, so that I
had nothing outwardly to help me, nor could tell what to do,
then, Oh then, I heard a voice which said, 'There is one,
even Christ Jesus, that can speak to thy condition,' and when

I heard it my heart did leap for joy. Then the Lord did let me see why there was none upon the earth that could speak to my condition, namely, that I might give him all the glory . . .

My desires after the Lord grew stronger, and zeal in the pure knowledge of God and of Christ alone, without the help of any man, book or writing. For though I read the Scriptures that spoke of Christ and of God, yet I knew him not but by revelation, as he who hath the key did open, and as the Father of life drew me to his Son by his spirit. And then the Lord did gently lead me along, and did let me see his love, which was endless and eternal, and surpasseth all the knowledge that men have in the natural state, or can get by history or books; and that love let me see myself as I was without him . . .

Yet I was under great temptations sometimes, and my inward sufferings were heavy; but I could find none to open my condition to but the Lord alone, unto whom I cried night and day . . . And I cried to the Lord, saying, 'Why should I be thus, seeing I was never addicted to commit those evils?' And the Lord answered that it was needful I should have a sense of all conditions, how else should I speak to all conditions; and in this I saw the infinite love of God. I saw also that there was an ocean of darkness and death, but an infinite ocean of light and love, which flowed over the ocean of darkness. And in that also I saw the infinite love of God; and I had great openings . . .

My sorrows and troubles began to wear off and tears of joy dropped from me, so that I could have wept night and day with tears of joy to the Lord, in humility and brokenness of heart. And I saw into that which was without end, and things which cannot be uttered, and of the greatness and infiniteness of the love of God, which cannot be expressed by words . . .

Now I was sent to turn people from darkness to the light that they might receive Christ Jesus, for to as many as should receive him in his light, I saw that he would give power to become the sons of God, which I had obtained by receiving Christ. And I was to direct people to the Spirit that gave forth the Scriptures, by which they might be led into all

Truth, and so up to Christ and God, as they had been who gave them forth. And I was to turn them to the grace of God, and to the Truth in the heart, which came by Jesus . . . I saw that the grace of God, which brings salvation, had appeared to all men, and that the manifestation of the Spirit of God was given to every man to profit withal. These things I did not see by the help of man, nor by the letter, though they are written in the letter, but I saw them in the light of the Lord Jesus Christ, and by his immediate Spirit and power, as did the holy men of God, by whom the Holy Scriptures were written.

The Journal of George Fox

Dear Friends, prize your time and the love of the Lord to your souls above all things, and mind that Light in you that shews you sin and evil. Which checks you when ye speak an evil word, and tells you that you should not be proud, nor wanton, nor fashion yourselves like unto the world; for the fashion of this world passeth away. And if ye hearken to that, it will keep you in humbleness of mind, and lowliness of heart, and turn your minds within, to wait upon the Lord, to be guided by it; and bring you to lay aside all sin and evil, and keep you faithful to the Lord; and bring you to wait upon him for teaching, till an entrance thereof be made to your souls, and refreshment come to them from the presence of the Lord. There is your Teacher, the Light, obeying it; there is your condemnation, disobeying it. If ye hearken to the Light in you, it will not suffer you to conform to the evil ways, customs, fashions, delights and vanities of the world; and so lead you to purity, to holiness, to uprightness, even up to the Lord.

Dear hearts, hearken to it, to be guided by it; for if ye love the Light, ye love Christ; if ye hate that, ye hate Christ. Therefore in the name of the Lord Jesus Christ consider of it; and the Lord open your understandings to know him!

Epistle 17 (1652)

John Aubrey
1626–1697

It is to Aubrey's disorganised heap of biography, anecdote, observation and gossip that we owe much of our information about his contemporaries. His eye for the trivial and the entertaining help to correct the impression of his subjects we might get from their own writings – always supposing that he's being accurate . . .

Thomas More

In his *Utopia* his law is that the young people are to see each other stark naked before marriage. Sir William Roper, of Eltham, in Kent, came one morning, pretty early, to my Lord, with a proposal to marry one of his daughters. My Lord's daughters were then both together abed in a truckle-bed in their father's chamber asleep. He carries Sir William into the chamber and takes the sheet by the corner and suddenly whips it off. They lay on their backs, and their smocks up as high as their arm-pits. This awakened them, and immediately they turned on their bellies. Quoth Roper, I have seen both sides, and so gave a pat on the buttock he made a choice of, saying, Thou art mine. Here was all the trouble of wooing . . .

After he was beheaded, his trunk was interred in Chelsea church, near the middle of the south wall, where there was some slight monument erected. His head was upon London Bridge. There goes this story in the family, viz, that one day as one of his daughters was passing under the bridge, looking on her father's head, said she, That head has lain many a time in my lap, would to God it would fall into my lap as I pass under. She had her wish, and it did fall into her lap, and is now preserved in a vault in the Cathedral Church at Canterbury.

The descendant of Sir Thomas, is Mr More, of Chilston, in Herefordshire, where, among a great many things of value plundered by the soldiers, was his chap [jawbone], which they kept for a relic. Methinks 'tis strange that all this time he is not canonised, for he merited highly of the Church. [More was canonised in 1935.]

Lancelot Andrewes

There was then at Cambridge a good fat alderman that was wont to sleep at church, which the alderman endeavoured to prevent but could not. Well! this was preached against as a sign of reprobation. The good man was exceedingly troubled at it, and went to Andrewes his chamber to be satisfied in point of conscience. Mr Andrewes told him, that it was an ill habit of body, not of mind, and that it was against his will; advised him on Sundays to make a more sparing meal, and to mend it at supper. The alderman did so, but sleep comes on again for all that, and was preached at; comes again to be resolved with tears in his eyes. Andrewes then told him he would have him make a good heartie meal as he was wont to do, and presently [at once] take out his full sleep. He did so, came to St Mary's, where the preacher was prepared with a sermon to damn all who slept at sermon, a certain sign of reprobation. The good alderman, having taken his full nap before, looks on the preacher all sermon time, and spoiled the design. But I should have said that Andrewes was most extremely spoken against and preached against for offering to assoil or excuse a sleeper in sermon time. But he had learning and wit enough to defend himself.

John Milton

His harmonical and ingenious soul did lodge in a beautiful and well proportioned body . . . Of a very cheerful humour. He would be cheerful even in his gout-fits, and sing . . .

Temperate man, rarely drank between meals. Extreme pleasant in his conversation, and at dinner, supper, etc; but satirical . . .

Brief Lives

John Bunyan
1628–1688

100,000 copies of The Pilgrim's Progess *were sold in the ten years after Bunyan's death. Within fifty years the work had been translated into many languages including Polish and Walloon. This Bedford tinker's son, who did most of his writing while in prison, has done more to influence English spirituality than any of the mystical divines.*

Christian and Hopeful Cross the River and Reach the Celestial City.

Now I further saw that betwixt them and the gate was a river, but there was no bridge to go over, the river was very deep. At the sight therefore of this river, the Pilgrims were much stounded; but the men that went with them, said, 'You must go through, or you cannot come at the Gate . . .'

The Pilgrims, then, especially Christian, began to despond in his mind, and looked this way and that, but no way could be found by them, by which they might escape the river. Then they asked the men, if the waters were all of a depth? They said, No; yet they could not help them in that case, for said they: 'You shall find it deeper or shallower, as you believe in the King of the place.'

They then addressed themselves to the water; and entering, Christian began to sink, and crying out to his good friend Hopeful he said, 'I sink in deep Waters, the billows go over my head, all his waves go over me, *Selah* . . .'

Then I saw in my dream, that Christian was in a muse a while; to whom also Hopeful added this word, 'Be of good cheer, Jesus Christ maketh thee whole.' And with that, Christian brake out with a loud voice, 'Oh, I see him again! and he tells me, When thou passest through the waters, I will be with thee, and through the rivers, they shall not overflow thee.' Then they both took courage, and the enemy was after that as still as a stone, until they were gone over. Christian therefore presently found ground to stand upon; and so it followed that the rest of the river was but shallow. Thus they got over. Now upon the bank of the river, on the other side, they saw the two shining men again, who there waited for them. Wherefore being come up out of the river, they saluted them saying, 'We are ministering spirits, sent forth to minister for those that shall be heirs to salvation.' Thus they went along towards the gate. Now you must note that the City stood upon a mighty hill, but the Pilgrims went up that hill with ease, because they had these two men to lead them up by the arms; also they had left their mortal garments behind them in the river; for though they went in with them, they came out without them. They therefore went up here with much agility and speed though the foundation upon which the City was framed was higher than the clouds. They therefore went up through the regions of the air, sweetly talking as they went, being comforted, because they safely got over the river, and had such glorious companions to attend them.

The talk they had with the shining ones, was about the glory of the place, who told them, that the beauty, and the glory of it was inexpressible. 'There,' said they, 'is the Mount Sion, the heavenly Jerusalem, the innumerable company of angels, and the spirits of just men made perfect. You are going now,' said they, 'to the Paradise of God, wherein you shall see the Tree of Life, and eat of the never-fading fruits thereof: and when you come there you shall have white robes given you, and your walk and talk shall be every day with the King, even all the days of eternity. There you shall not see again such things as you saw when you were in the lower region upon the Earth, to wit, sorrow, sickness, affliction, and death, for the former things are passed away . . .'

The men then asked, 'What must we do in the holy place?' To whom it was answered, 'You must there receive the comfort of all your toil, and have joy for all your sorrow; you must reap what you have sown, even the fruit of all your prayers and tears, and sufferings for the King by the way. In that place you must wear crowns of gold, and enjoy the perpetual sight and visions of the Holy One, for there you shall see him as he is . . .'

There came out also at this time to meet them several of the King's trumpeters, clothed in white and shining raiment, who with melodious noises and loud, made even the Heavens to echo with their sound. These trumpeters saluted Christian and his fellow with ten thousand welcomes from the world; and this they did with shouting, and sound of the trumpet . . .

Now I saw in my dream, that these two men went in at the gate; and lo, as they entered, they were transfigured, and they had raiment put on that shone like gold. There was also that met them with harps and crowns, and gave to them; the harp to praise withal, and the crowns in token of honour. Then I heard in my dream that all the bells in the City rang again for joy, and that it was said unto them, 'Enter ye into the joy of your Lord.' I also heard the men themselves, that they sang with a loud voice, saying, 'Blessing, honour, glory, and power, be to him that sitteth upon the throne, and to the Lamb for ever and ever.'

Now just as the gates were opened to let in the men, I looked in after them; and behold, the City shone like the sun, the streets also were paved with gold, and in them walked many men, with crowns on their heads, palms in their hands, and golden harps to sing praises withal.

There were also of them that had wings, and they answered one another without intermission, saying, 'Holy, Holy, Holy, is the Lord.' And after that, they shut up the gates; which when I had seen, I wished myself among them.

The Pilgrim's Progress

The Pilgrim Song

Who would true Valour see,
Let him come hither;
One here will Constant be,
Come Wind, come Weather.
There's no Discouragement
Shall make him once Relent
His first avow'd Intent
To be a Pilgrim

Whoso beset him round
With dismal Stories,
Do but themselves Confound;
His strength the more is.
No Lyon can him fright,
He'll with a Giant fight,
But he will have a right
To be a Pilgrim

116

Hobgoblin, nor foul Fiend,
Can daunt his Spirit:
He knows, he at the end
Shall Life Inherit.
Then Fancies fly away,
He'll fear not what men say,
He'll labour Night and Day
                    To be a Pilgrim.

He Plays Tip Cat on Sunday

But the same day, as I was in the midst of a game of Cat,
and having struck it one blow from the hole, just as I was
about to strike it the second time, a Voice did suddenly dart
from Heaven into my soul, which said 'Wilt thou leave thy
sins and go to Heaven, or have thy sins and go to Hell?' At
this I was put to an exceeding maze. Wherefore, leaving my
Cat upon the ground, I looked up to Heaven, and was as if
I had, with the eyes of my understanding, seen the Lord Jesus
looking down upon me, as being very hotly displeased with
me, and as if he did severely threaten me with some grievous
punishment for these and other my ungodly practices.

I had no sooner thus conceived in my mind, but suddenly
this conclusion was fastened on my spirit (for the former hint
did set my sins again before my face), that I had been a great
and grievous sinner, and that it was now too late for me to
look after Heaven; for Christ would not forgive me, nor
pardon my transgressions. Then I fell to musing upon this
also. And while I was thinking on it and fearing lest it should
be so, I felt my heart sink in despair, concluding it was too
late; and therefore I resolved in my mind I would go on in
sin. For, thought I, if the case be thus, my state is surely
miserable. Miserable if I leave my sins, and but miserable if
I follow them. I can but be damned, and if I must be so, I
had as good be damned for many sins as be damned for few.

Thus I stood in the midst of my play, before all that then
were present; but yet I told them nothing. But I say, I having
made this conclusion, I returned desperately to my sport

117

again; and I well remember, that presently this kind of despair did so possess my soul, that I was persuaded, I could never attain to other comfort than what I should get in sin; for Heaven was gone already, so that on that I must not think.

Grace Abounding

Thomas Ken
1637–1711

Thomas Ken is known almost exclusively for the hymns given below, which he produced for Winchester College together with some prayers. Besides this, he spent some time in the Tower as a non-juring bishop and refused the use of his house to Nell Gwynne, the King's mistress, when the court visited Winchester.

Alas! our weakness is very great, our wants are very many, our dependence on God for all things, all our lives long, is entire, and absolute, and necessary, and there is no way in the world to gain help and supplies from God, but by prayer; so that it is as easy and as possible to preserve a natural life without daily bread, as a Christian life without daily prayer.

You cannot imagine the great benefit of learning psalms by heart; for when you are under any temptation, or are in any affliction, or when you lie waking in the night, or when sick, these psalms will come into your mind; and the devout repeating them, will yield you most seasonable consolations.

Directions for Prayer, for the Diocese of Bath and Wells

A Morning Hymn

Awake, my soul, and with the sun,
Thy daily stage of duty run;
Shake off dull sloth, and joyful rise,
To pay thy morning sacrifice.

In conversation be sincere,
Keep conscience as the noon-tide clear.
Think how all-seeing God thy ways,
And all thy secret thoughts surveys.

All praise to thee, who safe hast kept,
And hast refresh'd me whilst I slept:
Grant, Lord, when I from death shall wake,
I may of endless light partake.

I would not wake, nor rise again,
Even heaven itself I would disdain.
Wert not thou there to be enjoy'd,
And I in hymns to be employed.

Lord, I my vows to thee renew;
Disperse my sins as morning dew;
Guard my first springs of thought and will,
And with thyself my spirit fill.

Direct, control, suggest, this day,
All I design, or do, or say;
That all my powers with all their might,
In thy sole glory may unite.

An Evening Hymn

All praise to thee, my God, this night,
For all the blessings of the light.
Keep me, O keep me, King of kings,
Beneath thy own Almighty wings.

Forgive me, Lord, for thy dear Son,
The ill that I this day have done;
That with the world, myself, and thee,
I ere I sleep at peace may be.

Teach me to live, that I may dread
The grave as little as my bed;
Teach me to die, that so I may
Rise glorious on that awful day.

O may my soul on thee repose,
And may sweet sleep mine eyelids close;
Sleep that may me more vig'rous make,
To serve my God when I awake.

When in the night I sleepless lie,
My soul with heavenly thoughts supply;
Let no ill dreams disturb my rest,
No power of darkness me molest.

O may my Guardian while I sleep,
Close to my bed his vigils keep,
His love angelical instil,
Stop all the avenues of ill.

Hymns for the use of the Scholars of Winchester College

Thomas Traherne
1637–1674

Until the winter of 1896–97 Thomas Traherne was a forgotten cleric in seventeenth-century Herefordshire. But then W. T. Brooke bought an anonymous manuscript from a London bookstall. It contained Traherne's Centuries of Meditations *and many of his poems, and they were published for the first time in 1908. It was a happy find, since Traherne's exuberant delight in childhood and God's creation is unique in English literature.*

(25)

Your enjoyment of the World is never right, till you so esteem it, that everything in it, is more your treasure than a King's exchequer full of Gold and Silver. And that exchequer yours also in its place and service. Can you take too much joy in your Father's works? He is Himself in everything. Some things are little on the outside, and rough and common, but I remember the time when the dust of the streets were as precious as Gold to my infant eyes, and now they are more precious to the eye of reason.

(27)

You never enjoy the world aright, till you see how a sand exhibiteth the wisdom and power of God: and prize in everything the service which they do you, by manifesting His glory and goodness to your Soul, far more than the visible beauty on their surface, or the material services they can do your body. Wine by its moisture quencheth my thirst, whether I consider it or no: but to see it flowing from His love who gave it unto man, quencheth the thirst even of the Holy Angels.

To consider it, is to drink it spiritually. To rejoice in its diffusion is to be of a public mind. And to take pleasure in all the benefits it doth to all is Heavenly, for so they do in Heaven. To do so is to be divine and good, and to imitate our Infinite and Eternal Father.

(28)

Your enjoyment of the world is never right, till every morning you awake in Heaven; see yourself in your Father's Palace; and look upon the skies, the earth, and the air as Celestial Joys: having such a reverend esteem of all, as if you were among the Angels. The bride of a monarch, in her husband's chamber, hath no such causes of delight as you.

(29)

You never enjoy the world aright, till the Sea itself floweth in your veins, till you are clothed with the heavens, and crowned with the stars: and perceive yourself to be the sole heir of the whole world, and more than so, because men are in it who are every one sole heirs as well as you. Till you can sing and rejoice and delight in God, as misers do in gold, and Kings in sceptres, you never enjoy the world.

(31)

Yet further, you never enjoy the world aright, till you so love the beauty of enjoying it, that you are covetous and earnest to persuade others to enjoy it. And so perfectly hate the abominable corruption of men in despising it, that you had rather suffer the flames of Hell than willingly be guilty of their error. There is so much blindness and ingratitude and damned folly in it . . .

(34)

Would one think it possible for a man to delight in gauderies like a butterfly, and neglect the Heavens? Did we not daily see it, it would be incredible. They rejoice in a piece of gold more than in the Sun; and get a few little glittering stones and call them jewels. And admire them because they be resplendent like the stars, and transparent like the air, and pellucid like the sea. But the stars themselves which are ten thousand times more useful, great, and glorious they disregard. Nor shall the air itself be counted anything, though it be worth all the pearls and diamonds in ten thousand worlds.

121

A work of God so Divine by reason of its precious and pure transparency, that all worlds would be worth nothing without such a treasure.

(47)

To have blessings and to prize them is to be in Heaven; to have them and not to prize them is to be in Hell, I would say upon Earth: To prize them and not to have them, is to be in Hell. Which is evident by the effects. To prize blessings while we have them is to enjoy them, and the effect thereof is contentation, pleasure, thanksgiving, happiness. To prize them when they are gone, produceth envy, covetousness, repining, ingratitude, vexation, misery. But it was no great mistake to say, that to have blessings and not to prize them is to be in Hell. For it maketh them ineffectual, as if they were absent. Yea, in some respect it is worse than to be in Hell. It is more vicious, and more irrational.

Century I

(1)

Will you see the infancy of this sublime and celestial greatness? Those pure and virgin apprehensions I had from the womb, and that divine light wherewith I was born are the best unto this day, wherein I can see the Universe. By the Gift of God they attended me into the world, and by His special favour I remember them till now. Verily they seem the greatest gifts His wisdom could bestow, for without them all other gifts had been dead and vain. They are unattainable by book, and therefore I will teach them by experience. Pray for them earnestly: for they will make you angelical, and wholly celestial. Certainly Adam in Paradise had not more sweet and curious apprehensions of the world, than I when I was a child.

(2)

All appeared new, and strange at first, inexpressibly rare and delightful and beautiful. I was a little stranger, which at my entrance into the world was saluted and surrounded with innumerable joys. My knowledge was Divine. I knew by intuition those things which since my Apostasy, I collected again by the highest reason. My very ignorance was advantageous. I seemed as one brought into the Estate of Innocence. All things were spotless and pure and glorious: yea, and infinitely mine, and joyful and precious. I knew not that

122

there were any sins, or complaints or laws. I dreamed not of poverties, contentions or vices. All tears and quarrels were hidden from mine eyes. Everything was at rest, free and immortal. I knew nothing of sickness or death or rents or exaction, either for tribute or bread. In the absence of these I was entertained like an Angel with the works of God in their splendour and glory, I saw all in the peace of Eden; Heaven and Earth did sing my Creator's praises, and could not make more melody to Adam, than to me. All Time was Eternity, and a perpetual Sabbath. Is it not strange, that an infant should be heir of the whole World, and see those mysteries which the books of the learned never unfold?

(3)

The corn was orient and immortal wheat, which never should be reaped, nor was ever sown. I thought it had stood from everlasting to everlasting. The dust and stones of the street were as precious as gold: the gates were at first the end of the world. The green trees when I saw them first through one of the gates transported and ravished me, their sweetness and unusual beauty made my heart to leap, and almost mad with ecstasy, they were such strange and wonderful things. The Men! O what venerable and reverend creatures did the aged seem! Immortal Cherubims! And young men glittering and sparkling Angels, and maids strange seraphic pieces of life and beauty! Boys and girls tumbling in the street, and playing, were moving jewels, I knew not that they were born or should die; But all things abided eternally as they were in their proper places. Eternity was manifest in the Light of the Day, and something infinite behind everything appeared: which talked with my expectation and moved my desire. The city seemed to stand in Eden, or to be built in Heaven. The streets were mine, the temple was mine, the people were mine, their clothes and gold and silver were mine, as much as their sparkling eyes, fair skins and ruddy faces. The skies were mine, and so were the sun and moon and stars, and all the World was mine; and I the only spectator and I enjoyer of it. I knew no churlish proprieties, nor bounds, nor divisions: but all proprieties and divisions were mine: all treasures and possessors of them. So that with much ado I was corrupted, and made to learn the dirty devices of this world. Which now I unlearn, and become, as it were, a little child again that I may enter into the Kingdom of God.

Century III

John Arbuthnot
1667–1735

Originally physician to Queen Anne (until she died), Arbuthnot became a respected and much-loved member of the 'Scriblerus Club' with Swift and Pope. Swift declared 'he has more wit than we all have, and more humanity than wit'. He published his series of John Bull pamphlets in 1712, principally to complain about the war with France.

John Bull's Mother
[the Church of England]

John had a mother whom he loved and honoured extremely; a discreet, grave, sober, good-conditioned, cleanly old gentlewoman as ever lived; she was none of your cross-grained termagant, scolding jades, that one had as good be hanged as live in the house with, such as are always censuring the conduct and telling scandalous stories of their neighbours, extolling their own good qualities, and undervaluing those of others. On the contrary, she was of a meek spirit, and, as she was strictly virtuous herself, so she always put the best construction upon the words and actions of her neighbours, except where they were irreconcilable to the rules of honesty and decency. She was neither one of your precise prudes, nor one of your fantastical old belles, that dress themselves like girls of fifteen; as she neither wore a ruff, forehead cloth, nor high-crowned hat, so she had laid aside feathers, flowers, and crimpt petticoats. She scorned to patch and paint, yet she loved to keep her hands and her face clean. Though she wore no flaunting laced ruffles, she would not keep herself in a constant sweat with greasy flannel; though her hair was not stuck with jewels, she was not ashamed of a diamond cross: she was not, like some ladies, hung about with toys and trinkets, tweezer-cases, pocket-glasses, and essence-bottles; she used only a gold watch and an almanac, to mark the hours and the holidays.

Her furniture was neat and genteel, well fancied, with a *bon goût*. As she affected not the grandeur of a state with a canopy, she thought there was no offence in an elbow-chair; She had laid aside your carving, gilding, and japan work as being too apt to gather dirt; but she never could be prevailed upon to part with plain wainscot and clean hangings. There are some ladies that affect to smell a stink in everything; they are always highly perfumed, and continually burning frankincense in their rooms; she was above such affectation, yet she never would lay aside the use of brooms and scrubbing-brushes, and scrupled not to lay her linen in fresh lavender. She was no less genteel in her behaviour, well-bred, without affectation, in the due mean between one of your affected courtesying pieces of formality, and your romps that have no regard to the common rules of civility. There are some ladies that affect a mighty regard for their relations: we must not eat to-day for my uncle Tom; or my cousin Betty died this time ten years; let's have a ball to-night, it is my neighbour such-a-one's birthday. She looked upon all this as grimace, yet she constantly observed her husband's birthday, her wedding-day, and some few more. Though she was a truly good woman, and had a sincere motherly love for her son John, yet there wanted not those who endeavoured to create a misunderstanding between them, and they had so far prevailed with him once that he turned her out of doors [i.e. in 1643–60], to his great sorrow, as he found afterwards, for his affairs went on at sixes and sevens.

She was no less judicious in the turn of her conversation and choice of her studies, in which she far exceeded all her sex; your rakes that hate the company of all sober grave gentlewomen would bear hers; and she would, by her handsome manner of proceeding, sooner reclaim them than some that were more sour and reserved. She was a zealous preacher up of chastity and conjugal fidelity in wives, and by no means a friend to the newfangled doctrine of the indispensable duty of cuckoldom; though she advanced her opinions with a becoming assurance, yet she never ushered them in, as some

125

positive creatures will do, with dogmatical assertions – this is infallible, I cannot be mistaken, none but a rogue can deny it. It has been observed that such people are oftener in the wrong than anybody. Though she had a thousand good qualities, she was not without her faults, amongst which one might perhaps reckon too great lenity to her servants, to whom she always gave good counsel, but often too gentle correction.

Joseph Addison
1672–1719

Addison was a prolific writer, which he combined with a successful political career. Popular in his lifetime, he is today seldom read, since his chosen form was the now unfashionable essay. He was perhaps more optimistic about eighteenth-century society than many of his contemporaries, his Spectator *pieces persuading through gentle irony and wit rather than ridicule and invective.*

Sir Roger at Church

I am always very well pleased with a country Sunday; and think, if keeping holy the Seventh Day were only a human institution, it would be the best method that could have been thought of for the polishing and civilising of Mankind. It is certain the country people would soon degenerate into a kind of savages and barbarians, were there not such frequent returns of a stated time, in which the whole village meet together with their best faces, and in their cleanliest habits, to converse with one another upon indifferent subjects, hear their duties explained to them, and join together in adoration of the Supreme Being. Sunday clears away the rust of the whole week, not only as it refreshes in the minds the notions of religion, but as it puts both the sexes upon appearing in their most agreeable forms, and exerting all such qualities as are apt to give them a figure in the eye of the village . . .

As Sir Roger is Landlord to the whole congregation, he keeps them in very good order, and will suffer no body to sleep in it besides himself; for if by chance he has been surprised into a short nap at sermon, upon recovering out of it he stands up and looks about him, and if he sees any body else nodding, either wakes them himself, or sends his servants to them. Several other of the old knight's particularities break out upon these occasions: sometimes he will be lengthening out a verse in the singing-psalms, half a minute after the rest of the congregation have done with it; sometimes, when he is pleased with the matter of his devotion, he pronounces *Amen* three or four times to the same prayer; and sometimes stands up when every body else is upon their knees, to count the congregation, or see if any of his tenants are missing.

I was yesterday very much surprised to hear my old friend, in the midst of the service, calling out to one John Matthews to mind what he was about and not disturb the congregation. This John Matthews it seems is remarkable for being an idle fellow, and at that time was kicking his heels for his diversion. This authority of the knight, though exerted in that odd manner which accompanies him in all circumstances of life, has a very good effect upon the parish, who are not polite enough to see any thing ridiculous in his behaviour; besides that, the general good sense and worthiness of his character, make his friends observe these little singularities as foils that rather set off than blemish his good qualities.

As soon as the sermon is finished, no body presumes to stir till Sir Roger is gone out of the church. The knight walks down from his seat in the chancel between a double row of his tenants, that stand bowing to him on each side; and every now and then enquires how such an one's wife, or mother, or son, or father do whom he does not see at church; which is understood as a secret reprimand to the person that is absent.

The Spectator, no. 112

The Spacious Firmament on High

The spacious firmament on high,
With all the blue ethereal sky,
And spangled heavens, a shining frame,
Their great Original proclaim.
The unwearied sun from day to day
Does his Creator's power display,
And publishes to every land,
The works of an almighty hand.

127

Soon as the evening shades prevail
The moon takes up the wondrous tale,
And nightly to the listening earth
Repeats the story of her birth;
Whilst all the stars that round her burn
And all the planets in their turn,
Confirm the tidings, as they roll,
And spread the truth from pole to pole.

What though in solemn silence all
Move round the dark terrestial ball;
What though nor real voice nor sound
Amid their radiant orbs be found;
In reason's ear they all rejoice,
And utter forth a glorious voice;
For ever singing as they shine,
'The hand that made us is divine.'

Isaac Watts
1674–1748

Watts' career as a non-conformist preacher was cut short by ill-health and he spent the last half of his life in the house of a kind patron. The 500 hymns he wrote injected some much-needed poetry into Puritan church services. Dr Johnson said: 'He shewed them that zeal and purity might be expressed and enforced by polished diction.'

The Gift of Prayer

The gift of prayer is one of the noblest and most useful in the Christian life, and therefore to be sought with earnest desire and diligence; and in order to attain it, we must avoid these two extremes:

I   A confining ourselves entirely to precomposed forms of prayer.

II An entire dependence on sudden motions and suggestions of thought . . .

Do not affect to pray long, for the sake of length, or to stretch out your matter by labour and toil of thought, beyond the furniture of your own spirit. God is not the more pleased with prayers, merely because they are long, nor are Christians ever the more edified. It is much better to make up by the frequency of our devotions what we want in the length of them, when we feel our spirits dry, and our hearts straitened. We may also cry to God for the aids of His own Holy Spirit, even in the middle of our prayer, to carry us forward in that work: but every man is not fit to pray long. God has bestowed a variety of natural, as well as spiritual talents and gifts upon men; nor is the best Christian, or a saint of the greatest gifts, always fit for long prayers.

The Grace of Prayer

Prayer is a retirement from earth, and a retreat from our fellow creatures to attend on God, and hold correspondence with Him that dwells in Heaven. If our thoughts are full of corn and wine and oil, and the business of this life, we shall not seek so earnestly the favour and face of God, as becomes devout worshippers. The things of the world therefore must be commanded to stand by for a season, and to abide at the foot of the mount, while we walk up higher to offer up our sacrifices, as Abraham did, and to meet our God. Our aims, and ends, and desires should grow more spiritual, as we proceed in this duty. And though God indulges us to converse with Him about many of our temporal affairs in prayer, yet let us take care that the things of our souls, and the eternal world, always possess the chief room in our hearts . . .

Seek earnestly a state of friendship with Him with whom you converse, and labour after a good hope and assurance of that friendship. How unspeakable is the pleasure in holding converse with so infinite, so almighty, and so compassionate a Friend! And how ready will all the powers of nature be to render every honour to him, while we feel and know ourselves to be His favourites, and the children of His grace?

A Guide to Prayer

When I survey

When I survey the wond'rous Cross
Where the young Prince of Glory dy'd,
My richest Gain I count but Loss,
And pour Contempt on all my Pride.

129

Forbid it, Lord, that I should boast
Save in the Death of *Christ* my God;
All the vain things that charm me most,
I sacrifice them to his Blood.

See from his Head, his Hands, his Feet,
Sorrow and Love flow mingled down;
Did e'er such Love and Sorrow meet?
Or Thorns compose so rich a Crown?

His dying Crimson like a Robe
Spreads o'er his Body on the Tree,
Then am I dead to all the Globe,
And all the Globe is dead to me.

Were the whole Realm of Nature mine,
That were a Present far too small;
Love so amazing, so divine
Demands my Soul, my Life, my All.

Man has a Soul of vast Desires

Man has a Soul of vast Desires,
He burns within with restless Fires,
Tost to and fro his Passions fly
From Vanity to Vanity.

In vain on Earth we hope to find
Some solid Good to fill the Mind,
We try new Pleasures, but we feel
The inward Thirst and Torment still.

So when a raging Fever burns
We shift from side to side by turns,
And 'tis a poor Relief we gain
To change the Place but keep the Pain.

Great God, subdue this vicious Thirst,
This Love to Vanity and Dust;
Cure the vile Fever of the Mind,
And feed our Souls with Joys refin'd.

from **Hymn XXX**

The Sorrows of the Mind
Be banisht from the Place!
Religion never was design'd
To make our Pleasures less.

Hymns and Spiritual Songs

William Law
1686–1761

Law's writings divide into two parts, the argumentative and the mystical. The first, including A Serious Call to a Devout and Holy Life, *made him popular with all but the moral hypocrites he attacked, and his circle of admirers included John Wesley. Later, when living a life of retirement as a sort of chaplain to two devout ladies near Stamford, his writings were heavily influenced by the German dualist Jacob Boehme.*

We readily acknowledge that God alone is to be the rule and measure of our prayers, that in them we are to look wholly unto him, and act wholly for him, that we are only to pray in such a manner, for such things and such ends as are suitable to his glory.

Now let anyone but find out the reason why he is to be thus strictly pious in his prayers, and he will find the same as strong a reason to be as strictly pious in all the other parts of his life. For there is not the least shadow of a reason, why we should make God the rule and measure of our prayers, why we should then look wholly unto him and pray according to his will, but what equally proves it necessary for us to look wholly unto God and make him the rule and measure of all other actions of our life. For any ways of life, any employment of our time or money, that is not strictly according to the will of God, that is not for such ends as are suitable to his glory, are as great absurdities and failings as prayers that are not according to the will of God . . .

131

Julius is very fearful of missing prayers; all the parish supposes Julius to be sick if he is not at church. But if you was to ask him why he spends the rest of his time by humour and chance? Why he is the companion of the silliest people in their most silly pleasures? . . . If you ask him why he never puts his conversation, his time, and fortune under the rule of religion, Julius has no more to say for himself than the most disorderly person. For the whole tenor of Scripture lies as directly against such a life, as against debauchery and intemperance.

Flavia and Miranda are two maiden sisters, that have each two hundred pounds a year. They buried their parents twenty years ago and have since that time spent their estate as they pleased.

Flavia has been the wonder of her friends, for her excellent management in making so surprising a figure in so moderate a fortune. She has everything that is in the fashion and is in every place where there is any diversion. Flavia is very orthodox, she talks warmly against heretics and schismatics, is generally at church and often at the sacrament. She once commended a sermon that was against the pride and vanity of dress, and thought it was very just against Lucinda, whom she takes to be a great deal finer than she needs to be.

If anyone asks Flavia to do something in charity, if she likes the person who makes the proposal, or happens to be in the right temper, she will toss him half a crown or a crown and tell him, if he knew what a long milliner's bill she had just received, he would think it a great deal for her to give. A quarter of a year after this, she hears a sermon upon the necessity of charity. She thinks the man preaches well, that it is a very proper subject, that people want much to be put in mind of it; but she applies nothing to herself, because she remembers that she gave a crown some time ago, when she could so ill spare it.

She will sometimes read a book of piety, if it is a short one, if it is much commended for style and language, and she can tell where to borrow it . . .

Miranda is a sober, reasonable Christian. As soon as she was mistress of her time and fortune, it was her first thought, how she might best fulfil everything that God required of her in the use of them, and how she might make the best and happiest use of this short life.

Miranda does not divide her duty between God, her neighbour and herself but considers all as due to God, and so does every thing in his name and for his sake. This makes her consider her fortune as the gift of God, to be used as every thing is that belongs to God, for the wise and reasonable ends of a Christian and holy life.

Her fortune therefore, is divided between herself and several other poor people. She thinks it the same folly to indulge herself in needless, vain expenses, as to give to other people to spend in the same way. Therefore she will not give a poor man money to go see a puppet show, but neither will she allow herself any to spend in the same manner, thinking it very proper to be as wise herself, as she expects poor men should be.

She is sometimes afraid that she lays out too much money in books, because she cannot forbear buying all practical books of any note, especially such as enter into the heart of religion, and describe the inward holiness of the Christian life. But of all human writings, the lives of pious persons and eminent saints are her greatest delight. In these she searches as for hidden treasure, hoping to find some secret of holy living, some uncommon degree of piety, which she might make her own.

Every one can tell how good and pious he would have some people to be; every one knows how wise and reasonable a thing it is in a bishop to be entirely above the world, and be an eminent example of Christian perfection. As soon as you think of a wise and ancient bishop, you fancy some exalted degree of piety, a living example of all those holy tempers which you find described in the Gospel.

Now, if you ask yourself, what is the happiest thing for a young clergyman to do? You must be forced to answer, that nothing can be so happy and glorious for him as to be like that excellent, holy bishop.

If you go on and ask what is the happiest thing for any young gentleman or his sisters to do? The answer must be the same: that nothing can be so happy or glorious for them as to live in such habits of piety, in such exercises of a divine life, as this good old bishop does. For every thing that is great and glorious in religion is as much the true glory of every man or woman, as it is the glory of any bishop. If high degrees of divine love, if fervent charity, if spotless purity, if heavenly affection, if constant mortification, if frequent devotion be the best and happiest way of life for any Christian, it is so for every Christian . . .

Apply this reasoning to yourself; if you find yourself living an idle, indulgent, vain life, choosing rather to gratify your passions than to live up to the doctrines of Christianity, and practise the plain precepts of our blessed Lord, you have all that blindness and unreasonableness to charge upon yourself that you can charge upon any irregular bishop.

This is the state of man, born with few wants and into a very large world very capable of supplying them. So that one would reasonably suppose, that men should pass their lives in content and thankfulness to God, at least that they should be free from violent disquiets and vexations, as being placed in a world that has more than enough to relieve all their wants.

But if to all this we add, that this short life, thus furnished with all that we want in it, is only a short passage to eternal glory where we shall be clothed with the brightness of angels, and enter into the joys of God, we might still more reasonably expect that human life would be a state of peace, and joy and delight in God. Thus it would certainly be, if reason had its full power over us.

But alas, though God and Nature and Reason make human life thus free from wants and so full of happiness, yet our passions, in rebellion against God, against Nature and against Reason, create a new world of evils, and fill human life with imaginary wants and vain disquiets.

I take it for granted, that every Christian that is in health is up early in the morning; for it is much more reasonable to suppose a person up early because he is a Christian than because he is a labourer, or a tradesman, or a servant, or has business that wants him.

A Serious Call to a Devout and Holy Life

It is a glorious and joyful truth (however suppressed in various systems of divinity) that from eternity to eternity no spark of wrath ever was or ever will be in the holy triune God. If a wrath of God was anywhere it must be everywhere; if it burned once it must burn to all eternity. For everything that is in God Himself is boundless, incapable of any increase or diminution, without beginning and without end . . .

God, considered in Himself, is as infinitely separate from all possibility of doing hurt or willing pain to any creature as He is from a possibility of suffering pain or hurt from the hand of a man. And this, for the plain reason, because He is in Himself, in His Holy Trinity, nothing else but the boundless abyss of all that is good, and sweet, and amiable, and therefore stands in the utmost contrariety to everything that is not a blessing – in an eternal impossibility of willing and intending a moment's pain or hurt to any creature . . . As the sun has but one nature and can give forth nothing but the blessings of light, so the holy triune God has but one nature and intent towards all the creation, which is to pour forth the riches and sweetness of His divine perfections upon everything that is capable of them and according to its capacity to receive them.

The goodness of God breaking forth into a desire to communicate good was the cause and the beginning of the creation. Hence it follows that to all eternity God can have no thought or intent towards the creature but to communicate good; because He made the creature for this sole end, to receive good.

The Spirit of Prayer

Richard Challoner
1691–1781

The writings of Richard Challoner formed one of the chief sources of encouragement to beleaguered English Catholics well into this century. His translations include St Augustine, St Teresa, Thomas à Kempis and the Douai Bible, which became the standard Catholic version. But it was The Garden of the Soul *which taught his simple piety to nearly two centuries of ordinary Catholics.*

Mental Prayer

Meditation, consisting of Considerations on the great Truths of Christianity, pious Affections and manifold Elevations of the Soul to God, and serious Resolutions of devoting one's self to him, is allowed to be one of the most important Exercises of a Christian Life, and such as ought to be performed daily, by as many as would serve God in good earnest.

Lay up in your Mind such Points of your Meditation as have touched you most, and oftentimes in the Day reflect upon them. This compares to the gathering, as it were, a Nosegay, in this Garden of Devotion, to smell at all the Day.

Such as find Difficulty in Meditation, may help themselves by using some good books, reading leisurely, and pausing upon what they read, and drawing proper Affections and Resolutions from it.

Of your Work

In the midst of your Work, let your Interior, as much as possible, be taken up with God by Recollection: Make a Closet in your Heart for Jesus Christ, invite him in thither, and there entertain him as well as you can: Seat yourself with Magdalene at his Feet, and make frequent Aspirations of Love to him.

Recollection

By calling to mind, as often as you can in the Day, the Presence of God, represented as in the very centre of your Soul; making frequent Aspirations and Ejaculations of Love to him; offering frequently in the Day your whole Being, all the Powers of your Soul, and all your Senses and Faculties, with all your Thoughts, Words and Actions to him; and banishing, as much as you can, from you all vain Amusements, anxious Cares and irregular Affections; that so your Heart may easily find him, freely embrace him, and quietly respose in him.

The Garden of the Soul

Philip Dormer Stanhope (Earl of Chesterfield)
1694–1773

Johnson said of Chesterfield's Letters to his Son: *'They teach the morals of a whore and the manners of a dancing master.' In reality he was simply more honest than most in giving expression to the commonly held 'insurance policy' view of religion.*

London, January the 8th, O.S. 1750.

Dear Boy,

I have seldom or never written to you upon the subject of Religion and Morality: your own reason, I am persuaded, has given you true notions of both; they speak best for themselves; but, if they wanted assistance, you have Mr Harte at hand, both for precept and example: to your own reason, therefore, and to Mr Harte, shall I refer you, for the reality of both; and confine myself, in this letter, to the decency, the utility, and the necessity, of scrupulously preserving the appearances of both. When I say the appearances of religion, I do not mean that you should talk or act like a missionary, or an enthusiast, nor that you should take up a controversial cudgel, against whoever attacks the sect you are of; this would be both useless, and unbecoming your age: but I mean that you should by no means seem to approve, encourage, or applaud, those libertine notions, which strike at religions equally, and which are the poor thread-bare topics of half wits, and minute philosophers. Even those who are silly enough to laugh at their jokes, are still wise enough to distrust and detest their characters: for, putting moral virtues at the highest, and religion at the lowest, religion must still be allowed to be a collateral security, at least, to virtue; and every prudent man will sooner trust to two securities than to one.

Letters to his Son

Philip Doddridge
1702–1751

Doddridge was a devout non-conformist minister whose personal piety over-rode his Northampton congregation's suspicions about what seemed to them like religious tolerance (a very unpopular notion just then). His prose writings and hymns were well received, particularly his dramatic account of the conversion of a libertine solder, Col. James Gardiner. At the age of 49 he travelled to Lisbon for his health . . . and died on arrival.

I hope, my dear, you will not be offended when I tell you that I am, what I hardly thought it possible, without a miracle, that I should have been, very easy and happy without you. My days begin, pass, and end in pleasure, and seem short because they are so delightful. It may seem strange to say it, but really so it is, I hardly feel that I want anything. I often think of you, and pray for you, and bless God on your account, and please myself with the hope of many comfortable days, and weeks, and years with you; yet I am not at all anxious about your return, or indeed about anything else. And the reason, the great and sufficient reason, is, that I have more of the presence of God with me than I remember ever to have enjoyed in any one month of my life. He enables me to live for him, and to live with him. When I awake in the morning, which is always before it is light, I address myself to him, and converse with him, speak to him while I am lighting my candle and putting on my clothes, and have often more delight before I come out of my chamber, though it be hardly a quarter of an hour after my awaking, than I have enjoyed for whole days, or perhaps weeks of my life. He meets me in my study, in secret, in family devotions. It is pleasant to read, pleasant to compose, pleasant to converse with my friends at home; pleasant to visit those abroad – the poor, the sick; pleasant to write letters of necessary business by which any good can be done; pleasant to go out and preach the gospel to poor souls, of which some are thirsting for it, and others dying without it; pleasant in the week-day to think how near another Sabbath is; but, oh! much, much more pleasant, to think how near eternity is, and how short the journey through this wilderness, and that it is but a step from earth to heaven.

– from a letter to his wife (1742)

God of my Life

God of my life, through all my days
My grateful powers shall sound Thy praise;
My song shall wake with opening light,
And cheer the dark and silent night.

When anxious cares would break my rest,
And griefs would tear my throbbing breast,
Thy tuneful praises, raised on high,
Shall check the murmur and the sigh.

When death o'er nature shall prevail,
And all the powers of language fail,
Joy through my swimming eyes shall break,
And mean the thanks I cannot speak.

Happy Day

O happy day that fixed my choice
  On Thee, my Saviour and my God!
Well may this glowing heart rejoice,
  And tell its raptures all abroad.

Now rest, my long-divided heart;
  Fixed on this blissful centre, rest;
Nor ever from thy Lord depart,
  With Him of every good possessed.

John Wesley
1703–1791

John Wesley, at first an Anglican priest, founded the Methodist Society when the Anglican hierarchy closed its pulpits to him. His movement brought scriptural holiness back into English Christianity. Phenomenally active throughout his life, he travelled 250,000 miles and preached 40,000 sermons; his collected writings, which include everything from his famous journal to French grammars, stretch to 35 volumes.

All the time I was at Savannah I was beating the air. Being ignorant of the righteousness of Christ, which, by a living faith in him, bringeth salvation to everyone that believeth, I sought to establish my own righteousness, and so laboured in the fire all my days . . .

In this state I was indeed fighting continually, but not conquering. Before, I had willingly served sin; now it was unwillingly, but still I served it. I fell and rose and fell again. Sometimes I was overcome and in heaviness: sometimes I overcame and was in joy. For as in the former state I had some foretastes of the terrors of the law, so had I in this of the comforts of the Gospel. During this whole struggle between nature and grace which had now continued above ten years, I had many remarkable returns to prayer, especially when I was in trouble. I had many sensible comforts, which are indeed no other than short anticipations of the life of faith . . .

I continued to seek (though with strange indifference, dullness and coldness and unusually frequent lapses into sin) till Wednesday, May 24 [1738]. I think it was about five this morning, that I opened my Testament on those words, *there are given unto us exceeding great and precious promises, even that you should be partakers of the divine nature* (2 Peter 1:4). Just as I went out, I opened it again on those words, *You are not far from the kingdom of God* . . .

In the evening, I went very unwillingly to a society in Aldersgate Street, where one was reading Luther's *Preface to the Epistle to the Romans*. About a quarter before nine, while he was describing the change which God works in the heart through faith in Christ, I felt my heart strangely warmed. I felt I did trust in Christ, Christ alone for salvation; and an assurance was given me that he had taken away *my* sins, even *mine*, and saved *me* from the law of sin and death.

I began to pray with all my might for those who had in a more especial manner despitefully used me and persecuted me. I then testified openly to all there what I now first felt in my heart . . .

After my return home, I was much buffeted with temptations, but cried out and they fled away. They returned again and again. I as often lifted up my eyes and *he sent me help from his holy place*. And herein I found the difference between this and my former state chiefly consisted. I was striving, yea, fighting with all my might under the law, as well as under grace. But then I was sometimes, if not often, conquered; now, I was always conqueror.

The Journal of John Wesley

You do not at all understand my manner of life. Though I am always in haste, I am never in a hurry; because I never undertake any more work than I can go through with perfect calmness of spirit. It is true I travel four or five thousand miles in a year. But I generally travel alone in my carriage, and consequently am as retired ten hours in a day as if I was in a wilderness. On other days I never spend less than three hours (frequently ten or twelve) in the day alone. So there are few persons in the kingdom who spend so many hours secluded from all company. Yet I find time to visit the sick and the poor; and I must do it if I believe the Bible, if I believe these are the marks whereby the Shepherd of Israel will know and judge His sheep at the great day; therefore, when there is time and opportunity for it, who can doubt but this is matter of absolute duty? When I was at Oxford, and lived almost like an hermit, I saw not how any busy man could be saved. I scarce thought it possible for a man to retain the Christian spirit amidst the noise and bustle of the world. God taught me better by my own experience. I had ten times more business in America (that is, at intervals) than ever I had in my life. But it was no hindrance to silence of spirit.

– from a letter to Miss March, December 10, 1777

Be always ready to own any fault you have been in. If you have at any time thought, spoke, or acted wrong, be not backward to acknowledge it. Never dream that this will hurt the cause of God; no, it will further it. Be ever open and frank, when you are taxed with anything: Do not seek either to evade or disguise it. But let it appear just as it is, and you will thereby not hinder, but adorn the Gospel.

God's command, to *pray without ceasing*, is founded on the necessity we have of his grace, to preserve the life of God in the soul, which can no more subsist one moment without it than the body can without air.

Whether we think of or speak to God, whether we act or suffer for him, all is prayer, when we have no other object than his love, and the desire of pleasing him.

All that a Christian does, even in eating and sleeping, is prayer, when it is done in simplicity, according to the order of God, without either adding to or diminishing from it by his own choice.

Prayer continues in the desire of the heart, tho' the understanding be employed on outward things.

In souls filled with love, the desire to please God is a continual prayer.

It is good to renew ourselves from time to time by closely examining the state of our souls, as if we had never done it before. For nothing tends more to the full assurance of faith than to keep ourselves by this means in humility, and the exercise of all good works.

To continual watchfulness and prayer ought to be added continual employment. For grace fills a vacuum as well as nature, and the devil fills whatever God does not fill.

A Plain Account of Christian Perfection

Extract from the Covenant Service, first instituted by John Wesley in 1755, at which Methodists rededicate themselves to God (Wesley owes a large debt for the service to the seventeenth-century Puritans, Joseph and Richard Alleine):

Of old time the people called of God dedicated themselves to him in a Covenant of law and promise, the shadow of better things to come. We are called to a life in Christ, in whom we are redeemed from sin and consecrated to God, having been admitted into the New Covenant of love which our Lord instituted and sealed with his own blood, that it might remain forever.

On the one side this Covenant is the gracious promise of God in Christ, that he will fulfil in us, and for us, and through us, all that he has declared in Him who is the same yesterday, today, and forever . . .

On our part the Covenant means that we willingly engage ourselves to live no more unto ourselves, but to him who loved us and gave himself for us . . .

We know well that in the past we have not fulfilled all our part in this Covenant. We have been more willing to claim its promises than to be held by its bonds. We are ignorant and frail; too often we have been wayward and wilfully disobedient. Yet God has had long patience with us; his mercy endures forever . . .

And now, beloved, let us bind ourselves with willing bonds to our Covenant God, and take the yoke of Christ upon us.

This taking of his yoke upon us means that we are heartily content that he shall appoint us our place and work, and that he alone shall be our reward.

Christ has many services to be done; some are easy, others more difficult; some bring honour, others bring reproach; some are suitable to our natural inclinations and temporal interests, others are contrary to both. In some we may please Christ and please ourselves; but there are others in which we cannot please Christ except by denying ourselves. Yet the power to do this is assuredly given us in Christ. We can do all things in him who strengtheneth us.

Search your hearts, therefore, whether you can now freely

143

make a sincere and unreserved dedication of yourselves to God.

Make the Covenant of God your own. Engage yourself to him. Resolve to be faithful. Having engaged your heart to the Lord, resolve, not in your own strength, nor in the power of your own resolutions, but in his might, never to go back . . .

And here all the people shall join:

I am no longer my own, but yours. Put me to what you will, rank me with whom you will; put me to doing, put me to suffering; let me be employed for you or laid aside for you, exalted for you or brought low for you; let me be full, let me be empty; let me have all things, let me have nothing; I freely and heartily yield all things to your pleasure and disposal.

And now, O glorious and blessed God, Father, Son and Holy Spirit, you are mine, and I am yours. So be it. And the Covenant which I have made on earth, let it be ratified in heaven.

'A Service for such as would make or renew their Covenant with God' [a modern adaptation]

Charles Wesley
1707–1788

Charles was an able partner to his older brother John in the Methodist Movement, and he was a zealous member of the small Oxford group from which it sprang in the 1730s. His main contribution was the composition of hymns, said to number some 6,500, which manage to combine passion and mysticism within a strong biblical idiom.

Jesu, my Strength, my Hope

Jesu, my strength, my hope,
  On thee I cast my care,
With humble confidence look up,
  And know thou hear'st my prayer.
Give me on thee to wait,
  Till I can all things do,
On thee almighty to create,
  Almighty to renew.

I want a sober mind,
A self-renouncing will
That tramples down and casts behind
The baits of pleasing ill:
A soul inured to pain,
To hardship, grief, and loss,
Bold to take up, firm to sustain
The consecrated cross.

I want a godly fear,
A quick-discerning eye,
That looks to thee when sin is near
And sees the tempter fly;
A spirit still prepared
And armed with jealous care,
Forever standing on its guard,
And watching unto prayer.

I want a heart to pray,
To pray and never cease,
Never to murmur at thy stay,
Or wish my sufferings less.
This blessing above all,
Always to pray I want,
Out of the deep on thee to call,
And never, never faint.

I want a true regard,
A single, steady aim,
Unmoved by threat'ning or reward,
To thee and thy great name;
A jealous, just concern
For thine immortal praise;
A pure desire that all may learn
And glorify thy grace.

I rest upon thy Word,
The promise is for me;
My succour, and salvation, Lord,
Shall surely come from thee.
But let me still abide,
Nor from thy hope remove,

Till thou my patient spirit guide
Into thy perfect love.

O Thou Who Camest from Above

O thou who camest from above
The pure celestial fire t'impart,
Kindle a flame of sacred love
On the mean altar of my heart!

There let it for thy glory burn
With inextinguishable blaze,
And trembling to its source return
In humble love, and fervent praise.

Jesu, confirm my heart's desire
To work, and speak, and think for thee;
Still let me guard the holy fire,
And still stir up thy gift in me;

Ready for all thy perfect will,
My acts of faith and love repeat,
Till death thy endless mercies seal
And make the sacrifice complete.

Jesu, Lover of my Soul

Jesu, Lover of my soul,
Let me to thy bosom fly,
While the nearer waters roll,
While the tempest still is high:
Hide me, O my Saviour, hide,
Till the storm of life be past!
Safe into the haven guide,
Oh, receive my soul at last!

Other refuge have I none,
Hangs my helpless soul on thee;
Leave, ah! leave me not alone,
Still support and comfort me:
All my trust on thee is stayed,
All my help from thee I bring;

Cover my defenceless head
    With the shadow of thy wing.

from *'Wrestling Jacob'*

Come, O thou Traveller unknown,
   Whom still I hold, but cannot see,
My company before is gone,
   And I am left alone with thee,
With thee all night I mean to stay,
And wrestle till the break of day.

In vain thou strugglest to get free,
   I never will unloose my hold:
Art thou the Man that died for me?
   The secret of thy love unfold.
Wrestling I will not let thee go,
Till I thy name, thy nature know.

'Tis Love, 'tis Love! Thou diedst for me,
   I hear thy whisper in my heart.
The morning breaks, the shadows flee:
   Pure Universal Love thou art;
To me, to all, thy bowels move,
Thy nature and thy name is Love.

My prayer hath power with God; the Grace
   Unspeakable I now receive,
Through Faith I see thee face to face,
   I see thee face to face, and live:
In vain I have not wept, and strove,
Thy nature and thy name is Love.

Samuel Johnson
1709–1784

Johnson's spirituality is marked by a deep sense of despair at what he saw as his own lack of achievement. Any glimpse of his talents merely reinforced his view that (despite Herculean projects like his dictionary) he was wasting his life. The prayers he left behind him are full of penitence and his friends were unable to talk him out of such moods.

[At a tea party Johnson interrupts a guest who was discoursing on the subject of astrology:]

Dr Johnson surprised him not a little, by acknowledging with a look of horror, that he was much oppressed by the fear of death. The amiable Dr Adams suggested that God was infinitely good: JOHNSON, 'That he is infinitely good, so far as the perfection of his nature will allow, I certainly believe; but it is necessary for good upon the whole, that individuals should be punished. As to an *individual*, therefore, he is not infinitely good; and as I cannot be *sure* that I have fulfilled the conditions on which salvation is granted, I am afraid I may be one of those who shall be damned.' (Looking dismally.) DR ADAMS, 'What do you mean by damned?' JOHNSON (passionately and loudly), 'Sent to hell, Sir, and punished everlastingly.' DR ADAMS, 'I don't believe that doctrine.' JOHNSON, 'Hold, Sir: do you believe that some will be punished at all?' DR ADAMS, 'Being excluded from heaven will be a punishment; yet there may be no great positive suffering.' JOHNSON, 'Well, Sir, but if you admit of any degree of punishment, there is an end of your argument for infinite goodness simply considered; for infinite goodness would inflict no punishment whatever. There is not infinite goodness physically considered: morally there is.' BOSWELL, 'But may not a man attain to such a degree of hope as not to be uneasy from the fear of death?' JOHNSON, 'A man may have such a degree of hope as to keep him quiet. You see I am not quiet, from the vehemence with which I talk; but I do not despair.' MRS ADAMS, 'You seem, Sir, to forget the merits of our Redeemer.' JOHNSON, 'Madam, I do not forget the merits of my Redeemer; but my Redeemer has said that he will set some on his right hand and some on his left.' – He was in gloomy agitation, and said, 'I'll have no more on't.'

In 1777, it appears from his *Prayers and Meditations*, that Johnson suffered much from a state of mind 'unsettled and perplexed', and from that constitutional gloom which, together with his extreme humility and anxiety with regard to his religious state, made him contemplate himself through too dark and unfavourable a medium. It may be said of him, that he 'saw God in clouds'. Certain we may be of his injustice to himself in the following lamentable paragraph:

'When I survey my past life, I discover nothing but a barren waste of time, with some disorders of body, and disturbances of the mind very near to madness, which I hope He that made me will suffer to extenuate many faults, and excuse many deficiencies.'

Boswell's *The Life of Samuel Johnson*

He loved the poor as I never yet saw any one else do, with an earnest desire to make them happy. What signifies, says someone, giving halfpence to common beggars? They only lay it out in gin or tobacco. 'And why (says Johnson) should they be denied such sweeteners of their existence? it is surely very savage to refuse them every possible avenue to pleasure, reckoned too coarse for our own acceptance. Life is a pill which none of us can bear to swallow without gilding; yet for the poor we delight in stripping it still barer, and are not ashamed to show even visible displeasure, if ever the bitter taste is taken from their mouths.' In consequence of these principles he nursed whole nests of people in his house, where the lame, the blind, the sick, and the sorrowful found a sure retreat from all the evils whence his little income could secure them.

Piozzi's *Anecdotes*

Christopher Smart
1722–1771

An unbalanced mind blighted Smart's life and literary career. He was locked up in Bedlam when his insanity took what was considered an anti-social turn: he was drawn to public prayer and insisted others joined him whenever the compulsion overcame him. He recovered partially and wrote some of his finest poetry, but declined again and died in a debtors' prison.

Hymn 9
(Moderation)

Tho' I my party long have chose,
    And claim Christ Jesus on my side,
Yet will I not my peace oppose,
    By pique, by prejudice, or pride.

Blessed be God, that at the font
    My sponsors bound me to the call
Of Christ, in England, to confront
    The world, the flesh, the fiend and all.

And yet I will my thoughts suppress,
    And keep my tongue from censure clear;
The Jew, the Turk, the Heathen bless,
    And hold the plough and persevere.

There's God in ev'ry man most sure,
    And ev'ry soul's to Christ allied:
If fears deject, if hopes allure,
    If Jesus wept, and pray'd and died.

Hymn 26
(Mutual Subjection)

Some think that in the Christian scheme
    Politeness has no part;
That manners we should disesteem,
    And look upon the heart.

The heart the Lord alone can read,
  Which left us this decree,
That men alternate take the lead
  In sweet complacency.

When his Disciples great dispute
  Christ Jesus reconcil'd,
He made their sharp contention mute,
  By shewing them a child.

If I have got the greater share
  Of talents – I shou'd bow
To Christ, and take the greater care
  To serve and to allow.

This union with the grace empow'r
  More influence to supply;
Hereafter, he that lacks this hour,
  May be as great as I.

Hymns for the Amusement of Children

John Newton
1725–1807

Renowned as a slave trader turned clergyman, most of Newton's slaving days occurred after his conversion to Christianity; the inhumanity of the trade only sunk in slowly. Later he played a key part in the evangelical revival and became well-known through his letters and the hymns he published with William Cowper at Olney in Buckinghamshire.

Spiritual Blindness

Neither education, endeavours, nor arguments, can open the eyes of the blind. It is God alone, who at first caused light to shine out of darkness, who can shine into our hearts, 'to give us the light of the knowledge of the glory of God in the face of Jesus Christ'. People may attain some natural ideas of spiritual truths by reading books, or hearing sermons, and may thereby become wise in their own conceits; they may learn to imitate the language of an experienced Christian; but they know not what they say, nor whereof they affirm, and are distant from the true meaning of the terms, as a blind man, who pronounces the words *blue* or *red*, is from the ideas which those words raise in the mind of a person who can distinguish colours by his sight.

Family Worship

Though all times and seasons are alike to the Lord, and his ear is always open whenever we have a heart to call upon him; yet to *us* there is a peculiar suitableness in beginning and closing the day with prayer: in the morning, to acknowledge his goodness in our preservation through the night, and entreat his presence and blessing on our persons and callings in the course of the day; and at night to praise him for the mercies of the day past, to humble ourselves before him for what has been amiss, to wait on him for a renewed manifestation of his pardoning love, and to commit ourselves and our concerns to his care and protection while we sleep . . .

When husband and wife are happily partakers of the same faith, it seems expedient, and for their mutual good, that, besides their private devotions, and joining in family-prayer, they should pray together. They have many wants, mercies, and concerns, in common with each other, and distinct from the rest of the family. The manner in which they should improve a little time in this joint exercise cannot well be prescribed by a third person; yet I will venture to suggest one thing. I conceive that it may prove much to their comfort to pray alternately, not only the husband with and for the wife, but the wife with and for the husband.

What the Believer Can Attain to in this Life

When I was lately at Mr Cox's Museum, while I was fixing my attention upon some curious movements, imagining that I saw the whole of the artist's design, the person who showed it touched a little spring, and suddenly a thousand new and unexpected motions took place, and the whole piece seemed animated from the top to the bottom. I should have formed but a very imperfect judgement of it, had I seen no more than what I saw at first.

Submission to the Will of the Lord

The schemes we form look so plausible and convenient, that when they are broken we are ready to say, What a pity! We try again, and with no better success: we are grieved, and perhaps angry, and plan out another, and so on: at length, in a course of time, experience and observation begin to convince us, that we are not more able than we are worthy to choose aright for ourselves. Then the Lord's invitation to cast our cares upon him, and his promise to take care of us, appear valuable; and when *we* have done planning, *his* plan in our favour gradually opens, and he does more and better for us than we could either ask or think.

Letters of John Newton

Christ, my Life

If ask'd, what of Jesus I think?
Though still my best thoughts are but poor,
I say, He's my meat and my drink,
My life, and my strength, and my store;
My shepherd, my husband, my friend,
My Saviour from sin and from thrall;
My hope from beginning to end,
My portion, my Lord, and my all.

Amazing Grace

Amazing grace! (how sweet the sound!)
　　That sav'd a wretch like me!
I once was lost, but now am found,
　　Was blind, but now I see.

'Twas grace that taught my heart to fear,
　　And grace my fears reliev'd;
How precious did that grace appear,
　　The hour I first believ'd.

Through many dangers, toils and snares,
　　I have already come;
'Tis grace has brought me safe thus far,
　　And grace will lead me home.

The Lord has promis'd good to me,
 His word my hope secures;
He will my shield and portion be,
 As long as life endures.

Yea, when this heart and flesh shall fail.
 And mortal life shall cease;
I shall possess, within the vail,
 A life of joy and peace.

The earth shall soon dissolve like snow,
 The sun forbear to shine;
But God, who call'd me here below,
 Will be for ever mine.

William Cowper
1731–1800

Religion was not a great comfort to William Cowper. Nervous and fragile from childhood, he was plunged into deeper depression by his acquaintance with the evangelist John Newton, from whom he got the idea that he was irrevocably damned. Cowper's melancholia lasted throughout their collaboration on The Olney Hymns, *lifting temporarily when Newton moved to London, but later plaguing the poet till his death.*

Exhortation to Prayer

What various hindrances we meet
In coming to a mercy-seat!
Yet who that knows the worth of pray'r
But wishes to be often there?

Pray'r makes the dark'ned cloud withdraw,
Pray'r climbs the ladder Jacob saw,
Gives exercise to faith and love,
Brings ev'ry blessing from above.

Restraining pray'r, we cease to fight;
Pray'r makes the Christian's armour bright;
And Satan trembles, when he sees
The weakest saint upon his knees.

While Moses stood with arms spread wide,
Success was found on Israel's side;
But when thro' weariness they fail'd,
That moment Amalek prevail'd.

Have you no words? Ah, think again!
Words flow apace when you complain
And fill your fellow-creature's ear
With the sad tale of all your care.

Were half the breath thus vainly spent
To heav'n in supplication sent,
Your cheerful song would oft'ner be:
'Hear what the Lord has done for me!'

Lovest Thou Me?

Hark, my soul! it is the Lord;
'Tis thy Saviour, hear His word;
Jesus speaks, and speaks to thee,
'Say, poor sinner, lovest thou me?

'I deliver'd thee when bound,
And when bleeding, heal'd thy wound;
Sought thee wandering, set thee right,
Turn'd thy darkness into light.

'Can a woman's tender care
Cease towards the child she bare?
Yes, she may forgetful be,
Yet will I remember thee.

'Mine is an unchanging love,
Higher than the heights above.
Deeper than the depths beneath,
Free and faithful, strong as death.

'Thou shalt see my glory soon,
When the work of grace is done;
Partner of my throne shalt be; –
Say, poor sinner, lovest thou me?'

Lord, it is my chief complaint,
That my love is weak and faint;
Yet I love Thee and adore, –
Oh! for grace to love Thee more!

Temptation

The billows swell, the winds are high,
Clouds overcast my wintry sky;
Out of the depths to Thee I call, –
My fears are great, my strength is small.

O Lord, the pilot's part perform,
And guard and guide me through the storm;
Defend me from each threatening ill,
Control the waves, – say, 'Peace! be still.'

Amidst the roaring of the sea
My soul still hangs her hope on Thee;
Thy constant love, thy faithful care,
Is all that saves me from despair.

Dangers of every shape and name
Attend the followers of the Lamb,
Who leave the world's deceitful shore,
And leave it to return no more.

Though tempest-toss'd and half a wreck,
My Saviour through the floods I seek;
Let neither winds nor stormy main
Force back my shatter'd bark again.

The Olney Hymns

William Blake
1757–1827

Suspicious of his real and literary visions, Blake's contemporaries wrote him off as gifted but insane. In fact his mystical works, though undoubtedly obscure, form a consistent and genuinely prophetic attack on eighteenth-century materialism and the puritanical narrowness of established Christianity.

from 'Auguries of Innocence'

To see a world in a grain of sand,
And a heaven in a wild flower,
Hold infinity in the palm of your hand,
And eternity in an hour.
A robin redbreast in a cage
Puts all heaven in a rage.
A dove-house filled with doves and pigeons
Shudders hell through all its regions.
A dog starved at his master's gate
Predicts the ruin of the state.
A horse misused upon the road
Calls to heaven for human blood.
. . .

The poison of the snake and newt
Is the sweat of envy's foot.
The poison of the honey bee
Is the artist's jealousy.
The prince's robes and beggar's rags
Are toadstools on the miser's bags.
A truth that's told with bad intent
Beats all the lies you can invent.
It is right it should be so;
Man was made for joy and woe;
And when this we rightly know,
Through the world we safely go.
Joy and woe are woven fine,
A clothing for the soul divine;
Under every grief and pine
Runs a joy with silken twine.

157

I assert for myself that I do not behold the outward creation, and that to me it is a hindrance and not action ... 'What!' it will be questioned, 'when the sun rises do you not see a round disc of fire somewhat like a guinea?' 'Oh no, no: I see an innumerable company of the heavenly host crying, "Holy, holy, holy, is the Lord God Almighty." '

Writings

And Did Those Feet in Ancient Time

And did those feet in ancient time
Walk upon England's mountains green?
And was the holy Lamb of God
On England's pleasant pastures seen?

And did the Countenance Divine
Shine forth upon our clouded hills?
And was Jerusalem builded here
Among these dark satanic mills?

Bring me my bow of burning gold!
Bring me my arrows of desire!
Bring me my spear! O clouds unfold!
Bring me my chariot of fire!

I will not cease from mental fight,
Nor shall my sword sleep in my hand
Till we have built Jerusalem
In England's green and pleasant land.

William Wordsworth
1770–1850

Wordsworth, still considered the father-figure of the Romantic move-ment, wrote pages and pages of 'Ecclesiastical Sonnets' telling the history of the English Church. They are dreadful. He describes the gunpower plot, for instance, as 'the horrible catastrophe of an assembled Senate unredeemed from subterraneous Treason's darkling power'. His spiritual sense increased, however, the further he got away from the Church – a not uncommon experience.

from *'Ode on Intimations of Immortality'*

V

Our birth is but a sleep and a forgetting;
The Soul that rises with us, our life's Star,
    Hath had elsewhere its setting,
        And cometh from afar:
    Not in entire forgetfulness,
    And not in utter nakedness,
But trailing clouds of glory do we come
    From God, who is our home:
Heaven lies about us in our infancy!
Shades of the prison-house begin to close
    Upon the growing Boy
But he beholds the light, and whence it flows,
    He sees it in his joy;
The Youth, who daily farther from the east
    Must travel, still is Nature's Priest,
    And by the vision splendid
    Is on his way attended;
At length the Man perceives it die away,
And fade into the light of common day.

VI

Earth fills her lap with pleasures of her own;
Yearnings she hath in her own natural kind,
And, even with something of a Mother's mind,
    And no unworthy aim,
    The homely Nurse doth all she can

To make her Foster-child, her Inmate Man,
    Forget the glories he hath known,
And that imperial palace whence he came . . .

IX

    O joy! that in our embers
    Is something that doth live,
    That nature yet remembers
    What was so fugitive!
The thought of our past years in me doth breed
Perpetual benediction: not indeed
For that which is most worthy to be blest;
Delight and liberty, the simple creed
Of Childhood, whether busy or at rest,
With new-fledged hope still fluttering in his breast:
    Not for these I raise
    The song of thanks and praise;
    But for those obstinate questionings
    Of sense and outward things,
    Fallings from us, vanishings;
    Blank misgivings of a Creature
Moving about in worlds not realised,
High instincts before which our mortal Nature
Did tremble like a guilty Thing surprised:
    But for those first affections,
    Those shadowy recollections,
    Which, be they what they may,
Are yet the fountain-light of all our day,
Are yet a master-light of all our seeing;
    Uphold us, cherish, and have power to make
Our noisy years seem moments in the being
Of the eternal Silence: truths that wake,
    To perish never:
Which neither listlessness, nor mad endeavour,
    Nor Man nor Boy,
Nor all that is at enmity with joy,
Can utterly abolish or destroy!
    Hence in a season of calm weather
    Though inland far we be,
Our Souls have sight of that immortal sea

Which brought us hither,
   Can in a moment travel thither,
And see the Children sport upon the shore,
And hear the mighty waters rolling evermore . . .

Recollections of Early Childhood

Sydney Smith
1771–1845

Smith's political outspokenness – in fact, his outspokenness on every subject – kept him from the high office in the Church of England he deserved. Despite his sharp wit and his metropolitan tastes, he was a diligent rector in his northern parish of Foston, which was so remote that Smith, rather an epicure, grumbled that it was 'twelve miles from a lemon'.

—'s idea of heaven, is eating *patés de foie gras* to the sound of trumpets.

After visiting a Puritan family, Smith wrote:

I endeavoured in vain to give them more cheerful ideas of religion, to teach them, that God is not a jealous, childish, merciless tyrant; that he is best served by a regular tenor of good actions – not by bad singing, ill-composed prayers and eternal apprehensions. But the luxury of false religion is to be unhappy.

The observances of the Church concerning feasts and fasts are tolerably well kept upon the whole, since the rich keep the feasts and the poor the fasts.

Benevolence is a natural instinct of the human mind. When A sees B in grievous distress, his conscience always urges him to entreat C to help him.

It is a bore, I admit, to be past seventy, for you are left for execution and are daily expecting the death-warrant; but it

161

is not anything very capital we quit. We are, at the close of life, only hurried away from stomach aches, pains in the joints, from sleepless nights and unamusing days, from weakness, ugliness, and nervous tremors; but we shall all meet again in another planet, cured of all our defects. Rogers will be less irritable, Macaulay more silent, Hallam will assent, Jeffrey will speak slower, Bobus will be just as he is, I shall be more respectful to the upper clergy.

Sayings and letters from various sources

I would say to that Royal child, worship God by loving peace. It is not *your* humanity to pity a beggar by giving him food or raiment – *I* can do that; that is the charity of the humble and the unknown. Widen you your heart for the more expanded miseries of mankind – pity the mothers of the peasantry who see their sons torn away from their families, pity your poor subjects crowded into hospitals, and calling in their last breath upon their distant country and their young Queen; pity the stupid, frantic folly of human beings who are always ready to tear each other to pieces, and to deluge the earth with each other's blood. This is your extended humanity – and this the great field of your compassion.

Extinguish in your heart the fiendish love of military glory, from which your sex does not necessarily exempt you, and to which the wickedness of flatterers may urge you. Say upon your death-bed, 'I have made few orphans in my reign – I have made few widows – my object has been peace. I have used all the weight of my character, and all the power of my situation, to check the irascible passions of mankind, and to turn them to the arts of honest industry: this has been the Christianity of my thone, and this the gospel of my sceptre; in this way I have striven to worship my Redeemer and my judge.

Sermon giving advice to the new Queen, Victoria

Samuel Taylor Coleridge
1772–1834

'An archangel slightly damaged' was how Charles Lamb described Coleridge, summing up the poet's contradictory life of promise and under-achievement, radical Christian concern and laudanum-induced lethargy.

The Eolian Harp
[composed at Clevedon, Somersetshire]

My pensive Sara! thy soft cheek reclined
Thus on mine arm, most soothing sweet it is
To sit beside our cot, our cot o'ergrown
With white-flowered Jasmin, and the broad-leaved Myrtle,
(Meet emblems they of Innocence and Love!),
And watch the clouds, that late were rich with light,
Slow saddening round, and mark the star of eve
Serenely brilliant (such should wisdom be)
Shine opposite! How exquisite the scents
Snatched from yon bean-field! and the world so hushed!
The stilly murmur of the distant sea
Tells us of silence.

    And that simplest lute,
Placed length-ways in the clasping casement, hark!
How by the desultory breeze caressed,
Like some coy maid half yielding to her lover,
It pours such sweet upbraiding, as must needs
Tempt to repeat the wrong! And now, its strings
Boldlier swept, the long sequacious notes
Over delicious surges sink and rise,
Such a soft floating witchery of sound
As twilight Elfins make, when they at eve
Voyage on gentle gales from Fairy-Land,
Where Melodies round honey-dropping flowers,
Footless and wild, like birds of Paradise,
Nor pause, nor perch, hovering on untamed wing!
O! the one life within us and abroad,
Which meets all motion and becomes its soul,

'A light in sound, a sound-like power in light
Rhythm in all thought, and joyance every where –
Methinks, it should have been impossible
Not to love all things in a world so filled;
Where the breeze warbles, and the mute still air
Is Music slumbering on her instrument.

And thus, my love! as on the midway slope
Of yonder hill I stretch my limbs at noon,
Whilst through my half-closed eye-lids I behold
The sunbeams dance, like diamonds, on the main,
And tranquil muse upon tranquillity;
Full many a thought uncalled and undetained,
And many idle flitting phantasies,
Traverse my indolent and passive brain,
As wild and various as the random gales
That swell and flutter on this subject lute!

And what if all of animated nature
Be but organic harps diversely framed,
That tremble into thought, as o'er them sweeps
Plastic and vast, one intellectual breeze,
At once the Soul of each, and God of all?

But thy more serious eye a mild reproof
Darts, O beloved woman! nor such thoughts
Dim and unhallowed dost thou not reject,
And biddest me walk humbly with my God.
Meek daughter in the family of Christ!
Well hast thou said and holily dispraised
These shapings of the unregenerate mind;
Bubbles that glitter as they rise and break
On vain Philosophy's aye-babbling spring.
For never guiltless may I speak of him,
The Incomprehensible! save when with awe
I praise him, and with Faith that inly feels;
Who with his saving mercies healed me,
A sinful and most miserable man,
Wildered and dark, and gave me to possess
Peace, and this cot, and thee, dear honoured Maid!

John Keble
1792–1866

Keble grew up in a High Anglican family, in which the writings of such men as William Law and Jeremy Taylor provided the staple spiritual food. After a successful academic career he became a country parson at Hursley near Winchester. With Newman he inspired the Anglo-Catholic movement in the Church of England.

On Conquering Melancholy by Active Kindness to Others

My dear —

I am bound to thank you over and over again for your last letter; it was and is a real comfort to me: for I am tolerably sure you are in the right way; only don't dwell too much upon whatever may have been wrong: to some minds it may be necessary, but not to those who are in danger of becoming indolent by too much thinking about themselves: and when you find yourself, as I dare say you sometimes do, overpowered as it were by melancholy, the best way is to go out, and do something kind to somebody or other. Objects either rich or poor will generally present themselves in the hour of need to those who look for them in earnest, although Oxford is not perhaps the most convenient place to find them in. However there they surely are if you will take the trouble of looking for them, and perhaps that very trouble is in some sort an advantage in doing away a moody fit; although I always reckon it a great privilege of a country Parson that his resources in this way lie close at his own door.

Writing, too, I have known in many cases, a very great relief, but I almost doubt the expediency of preserving journals, at least of looking much back upon them; if one could summon resolution to do so, I fancy the best way would be to write on till one was a little unburthened, and then put one's confessions in the fire. But in all these things, of course no one can judge for his neighbour. And whatever you do, don't put your confessions to *me* in the fire; for it does my heart good to receive them: it makes me hope that I am sometimes useful, which is a sensation I don't very often experience.

To a Friend, Newly Ordained

My dear —

. . . I do not think the glory of God best promoted by a rigid abstinence from amusements, except they be either sinful in themselves, or carried to excess, or in some other way ministering occasion to sin. On the contrary, I believe that there is more charity lost, than there is sobriety gained, by any unnecessary appearance of austerity. Self-denial seems to mean, not going out of the world, but walking warily and uprightly in it. Nor can I well imagine any greater service to society than is rendered by him, who submits to its common routine, though something wearisome, for this very reason: lest he should offend his neighbours by unnecessary rigour.

To One in Distress for Past Sin

My dear —

. . . If evil thoughts occur in the night, rise and pray on your knees for a few moments: say, e.g. the 51st Psalm. Some *slight* bodily hardship is often useful, I believe, at such times. Be very careful about your fasting, whether in the way of penitence or precaution; it causes sometimes, especially when persons are unused to it, a kind of reaction very distressing. If you have reason to fear that, you had better use hard and unpleasant diet, instead of actually going without.

To a Young Lady, on Distractions

My dear Child (for so your letter even forces me to call you),

. . . Your failure of recollection in church is no new nor rare thing. In some respects it may be perhaps mended by mechanical helps – something equivalent to a Rosary as a kind of *memoria technica*. And you will remember Bp Taylor's advice, to gather up as it were all the meaning of the lost prayer into a hearty Amen at the end of it. Remember this too (which is in all the books, and I have no doubt it is quite true), that the hearty desire to be contrite is accepted as contrition, the hearty desire to believe as Faith.

166

To a Lady, on the Absence of Conscious Love and Devotion

My dear Child,

I am truly sorry to hear of your distress continuing, but I must put it to your own conscience, whether there is not in it somewhat of self-tormenting and wilful peevishness; and whether, *so far*, the remedy is not, by God's mercy, in your own power. I must beg you to ask yourself whether you are really endeavouring to shake off the morbid feelings which haunt you, as sincerely as you would endeavour to cure a tooth-ache.

Letters of Spiritual Counsel

from '*Morning*'

New every morning is the love
Our wakening and uprising prove;
Through sleep and darkness safely brought,
Restored to life, and power, and thought.

New mercies, each returning day,
Hover around us while we pray;
New perils past, new sins forgiven,
New thoughts of God, new hopes of heaven.

If on our daily course our mind
Be set to hallow all we find,
New treasures still, of countless price,
God will provide for sacrifice.

Old friends, old scenes, will lovelier be,
As more of heaven in each we see:
Some softening gleam of love and prayer
Shall dawn on every cross and care.

The trivial round, the common task,
Would furnish all we ought to ask;
Room to deny ourselves; a road
To bring us, daily, nearer God.

Only, O Lord, in Thy dear love
Fit us for perfect Rest above;
And help us, this and every day,
To live more nearly as we pray.

167

from *'Evening'*

Sun of my soul! Thou Saviour dear,
It is not night if Thou be near:
Oh, may no earth-born cloud arise
To hide Thee from Thy servant's eyes.

When with dear friends sweet talk I hold,
And all the flowers of life unfold:
Let not my heart within me burn,
Except in all I Thee discern.

When the soft dews of kindly sleep
My wearied eyelids gently steep,
Be my last thought, how sweet to rest
For ever on my Saviour's breast.

Abide with me from morn till eve,
For without Thee I cannot live:
Abide with me when night is nigh,
For without Thee I dare not die.

Watch by the sick: enrich the poor
With blessings from Thy boundless store:
Be every mourner's sleep to-night,
Like infant's slumbers, pure and light.

Come near and bless us when we wake,
Ere through the world our way we take:
Till in the ocean of Thy love
We lose ourselves in heaven above.

The Christian Year

Henry Frances Lyte
1793–1847

A Somersetshire man, Lyte actually worked as a clergyman in Devon-shire. He wrote some well-known English hymns, but was forever plagued by ill-health. 'Abide with me' was written on the Sunday evening on which he gave communion to his congregation for the last time before travelling to Nice, whence he never returned.

Abide with me

Abide with me; fast falls the eventide;
The darkness deepens; Lord, with me abide:
When other helpers fail, and comforts flee,
Help of the helpless, oh abide with me.

Swift to its close ebbs out life's little day;
Earth's joys grow dim, its glories pass away;
Change and decay in all around I see;
O thou who changest not, abide with me.

I need thy presence every passing hour;
What but thy grace can foil the tempter's power?
Who like thyself my guide and stay can be?
Through cloud and sunshine, Lord, abide with me.

I fear no foe with thee at hand to bless;
Ills have no weight, and tears no bitterness;
Where is death's sting? where, grave, thy victory?
I triumph still, if thou abide with me.

Hold thou thy cross before my closing eyes;
Shine through the gloom, and point me to the skies;
Heaven's morning breaks, and earth's vain shadows flee;
In life, in death, O Lord, abide with me.

John Henry Newman
1801–1890

Newman was in fact a retiring man. Just as well, since the storm of publicity – much of it critical – which broke on his conversion from Anglo- to Roman Catholicism was followed by years of suspicion and neglect from the Roman hierarchy. He was a prolific writer and is most famous for his poem The Dream of Gerontius *and the* Apologia – *his defence against a fierce personal attack by Charles Kingsley.*

It is always a refreshment to the mind, and elevates it, to enter a Church such as San Fidelio. It has such a sweet, smiling, open countenance – and the altar is so gracious and winning, standing out for all to see, to approach. The tall polished marble columns, the marble rails, the marble floor, the bright pictures, all speak the same language. And a light dome crowns the whole. Perhaps I do but follow the way of elderly persons, who have seen enough that is sad in life to be able to dispense with officious sadness – and as the young prefer autumn and the old spring, the young tragedy and the old comedy, so in the ceremonial of religion, younger men may have my leave to prefer Gothic, if they will but tolerate me in my weakness which requires the Italian. It is so soothing and pleasant, after the hot streets, to go into these delicate yet rich interiors, which are like the bowers of paradise, or an angel's chamber.

Letters

In the matter in question, that is conversion, my own feelings were not *violent*, but a returning to, a renewing of principles, under the power of the Holy Spirit, which I had already felt, and in a measure acted on when young.

Memoir

I felt then, and all along felt, that there was an intellectual cowardice in not having a basis in reason for my belief, and a moral cowardice in not avowing that basis. I should have felt myself less than a man, if I did not bring it out, whatever it was . . . Alas! it was my portion for whole years to remain without any satisfactory basis for my religious profession, in a state of moral sickness, neither able to acquiesce Anglicanism, nor able to go to Rome. But I bore it, till in course of time my way was made clear to me.

I had a dear and old friend, near his death . . . I had expected that his last illness would have brought light to my mind, as to what I ought to do. It brought none. I made a note, which runs thus: 'I sobbed bitterly over his coffin, to think that he left me still dark as to what the way of truth was, and what I ought to do in order to please God and fulfil His will.' I think I wrote to Charles Marriott to say, that at that moment, with the thought of my friend before me, my strong view in favour of Rome remained just what it was. On the other hand, my firm belief that grace was to be found in the Anglican Church remained too . . .

I could not continue in this state, either in the light of duty or of reason. My difficulty was this: I had been deceived greatly once; how could I be sure that I was not deceived a second time? I then thought myself right; how was I to be certain that I was right now? How many years had I thought myself sure of what I now rejected? how could I ever again have confidence in myself? As in 1840 I listened to the rising doubt in favour of Rome, now I listened to the waning doubt in favour of the English Church. To be certain is to know that one knows; what test had I, that I should not change again, after that I had become a Catholic? I had still apprehension of this, though I thought a time would come when it would depart. However, some limit ought to be put to these vague misgivings; I must do my best and then leave it to a higher power to prosper it. So, I determined to write an essay on Doctrinal Development; and then, if, at the end of it, my convictions in favour of the Roman Church were not weaker, to make up my mind to seek admission into her fold. I acted upon this resolution in the beginning of 1845, and worked at my essay steadily into the autumn . . . As I advanced, my view so cleared that instead of speaking any more of 'the Roman Catholics', I boldly called them Catholics. Before I got to the end, I resolved to be received, and the book remains in the state in which it was then, unfinished . . .

From the time that I became a Catholic, of course I have no further history of my religious opinions to narrate. In saying this, I do not mean to say that my mind has been idle, or that I have given up thinking on theological subjects; but that I have had no changes to record, and have had no anxiety of heart whatever. I have been in perfect peace and contentment. I have never had one doubt. I was not conscious to myself, on my conversion, of any difference of thought or of temper from what I had before. I was not conscious of firmer faith in the fundamental truths of revelation, or of more self-command; I had not more fervour; but it was like coming into port after a rough sea; and my happiness on that score remains to this day without interruption.

Apologia Pro Vita Sua

The Pillar of the Cloud

Lead, Kindly Light, amid the encircling gloom,
    Lead Thou me on!
The night is dark, and I am far from home –
    Lead Thou me on!
Keep Thou my feet; I do not ask to see
The distant scene; one step enough for me.

I was not ever thus, nor pray'd that Thou
    Shouldst lead me on.
I loved to choose and see my path, but now
    Lead Thou me on!
I loved the garish day, and, spite of fears,
Pride ruled my will: remember not past years.

So long Thy power hath blest me, sure it still
    Will lead me on,
O'er moor and fen, o'er crag and torrent, till
    The night is gone;
And with the morn those angel faces smile
Which I have loved long since, and lost awhile.

At Sea, June 16, 1833

May we, one and all, set forward with this season, when the Spirit descended, that so we may grow in grace, and in the knowledge of our Lord and Saviour! Let those who have had seasons of seriousness, lengthen them into a life; and let those who have made good resolves in Lent, not forget them in Easter-tide; and let those who have hitherto lived religiously, learn devotion; and let those who have lived in good conscience, learn to live by faith; and let those who have made a good profession, aim at consistency; and let those who take pleasure in religious worship, aim at inward sanctity; and let those who have knowledge, learn to love; and let those who meditate, forget not mortification. Let not this sacred season leave us as it found us, let it leave us not as children, but as heirs and as citizens of the kingdom of heaven.

'Christian Nobleness' (Whitsuntide sermon)

Frederick Denison Maurice
1805–1872

Maurice started life as a journalist, and then took orders and became chaplain at Guy's Hospital in London. Later he was appointed Professor of Divinity at King's College, London, but was sacked because he refuted the doctrine of everlasting punishment for the wicked. He founded the Christian Socialist Movement and the Working Men's College.

Since the new kingdom has been set up in the world, men are no longer to be taught that they are to seek God, if haply they may feel after him and find him; but they are to be told that God is seeking them; that he has revealed himself to them in the person of his Son; and that he has made a covenant with then, that they shall be to him children, that he will be to them a Father.

The spirit of man sighs after something higher than mere quietness of conscience and will not be satisfied till it be attained ... the understanding is outraged unless we acknowledge truths and mysteries which surpass it.

173

Communion with God, in the largest and fullest sense of that word, is not an instrument of attaining some higher end, but is itself the end to which he is leading his creatures, and after which his creatures . . . are secretly longing and crying and without which they cannot be satisfied.

We are not sent into the world to obtain a certain set of notions respecting ourselves and God, but that we may actually know ourselves and know him.

Human relationships are not artificial types of something divine, but are actually the means, and the only means through which man ascends to any knowledge of the divine.

Wherever there was a man who had sought to be a faithful husband, or father, or brother, or had been led to feel that he had violated these relations and to long for reformation – in him was the seed of a churchman – to him the Gospel came as most wonderful, yet not altogether strange tidings. As it was a message of forgiveness he wanted it; for he, feeling that he was in an order, had the sense of transgression. As it was the declaration of death to self, he received it; for self had been that which had hindered him from fulfilling his relations, and that out of which they were educating him. As it was the declaration of life in another, he embraced it; all his attachments had been foreshadowing it and preparing him for it.

No man has a right to say, 'My race is a sinful race,' even when he most confesses the greatness of his own sin and fall; because he is bound to contemplate his race in the Son of God, and to claim, by faith in him, his share in its redemption and its glory.

The Kingdom of Christ

Instead of resting on our own weak changeable wills, we shall trust ourselves and the universe to the perfect, holy, unchangeable will. We shall believe that we are only called out by him that we may declare his name, his kingdom, his redemption, to all people whatsoever.

The Faith and the Liturgy

Alfred Tennyson
1809–1892

In Memoriam – sixteen years in the making – was Tennyson's tribute to Arthur Hallam, a Cambridge friend who had died at the age of 22. Although it concludes with Hallam 'living in God', it passes through many dark passages getting him there, reflecting Tennyson's natural melancholy and his suspicion of the Victorian optimism he was supposed to represent.

from *'In Memoriam A.H.H.'*

LIV

Oh yet we trust that somehow good
    Will be the final goal of ill,
    To pangs of nature, sins of will,
Defects of doubt, and taints of blood;

That nothing walks with aimless feet;
    That not one life shall be destroy'd,
    Or cast as rubbish to the void,
When God hath made the pile complete;

That not a worm is cloven in vain;
    That not a moth with vain desire
    Is shrivell'd in a fruitless fire,
Or but subserves another's gain.

Behold, we know not anything;
    I can but trust that good shall fall
    At last – far off – at last, to all,
And every winter change to spring.

So runs my dream: but what am I?
    An infant crying in the night:
    An infant crying for the light:
And with no language but a cry.

XCVI

You say, but with no touch of scorn,
    Sweet-hearted, you, whose light-blue eyes

Are tender over drowning flies,
You tell me, doubt is Devil-born.

I know not: one indeed I knew
    In many a subtle question versed,
    Who touch'd a jarring lyre at first,
But ever strove to make it true:

Perplext in faith, but pure in deeds,
    At last he beat his music out.
    There lives more faith in honest doubt,
Believe me, than in half the creeds.

He fought his doubts and gather'd strength,
    He would not make his judgment blind,
    He faced the spectres of the mind
And laid them; thus he came at length

To find a stronger faith his own;
    And Power was with him in the night,
    Which makes the darkness and the light,
And dwells not in the light alone,

But in the darkness and the cloud,
    As over Sinai's peaks of old,
    While Israel made their gods of gold,
Altho' the trumpet blew so loud.

from *'The Passing of Arthur'*

King Arthur speaks:

'I found Him in the shining of the stars,
I mark'd Him in the flowering of His fields,
But in His ways with men I found Him not.
I waged His wars, and now I pass and die.
O me! for why is all around us here
As if some lesser god had made the world,
But not had force to shape it as he would,
Till the High God behold it from beyond,
And enter it, and make it beautiful?
Or else as if the world were wholly fair,
But that these eyes of men are dense and dim,

And have not power to see it as it is:
Perchance, because we see not to the close;
For I, being simple, thought to work His will,
And have but stricken with the sword in vain;
And all whereon I lean'd in wife and friend
Is traitor to my peace, and all my realm
Reels back into the beast, and is no more.
My God, thou hast forgotten me in my death:
Nay – God my Christ – I pass but shall not die . . .

The old order changeth, yielding place to new,
And God fulfils himself in many ways,
Lest one good custom should corrupt the world.
Comfort thyself: what comfort is in me?
I have lived my life, and that which I have done
May He within himself make pure! but thou,
If thou shouldst never see my face again,
Pray for my soul. More things are wrought by prayer
Than this world dreams of. Wherefore, let thy voice
Rise like a fountain for me night and day.
For what are men better than sheep or goats
That nourish a blind life within the brain,
If, knowing God, they lift not hands of prayer
Both for themselves and those who call them friend?
For so the whole round earth is every way
Bound by gold chains about the feet of God.'

Robert Browning
1812–1889

*Browning is now very little read, but, after an insignificant beginning,
he became the most loved poet of the late Victorians and the Edwardians.
This regard was not hindered in any way by his romantic marriage
with Elizabeth Barrett. Much influenced by his Nonconformist mother,
Browning attacked religious cant and his poetry displays a robust,
questioning, man-of-the-world faith.*

from 'Bishop Blougram's Apology'

[The Bishop defends his faith and status to a sceptical journalist:]

> . . . Our dogmas then
> With both of us, though in unlike degree,
> Missing full credence – overboard with them!
> I mean to meet you on your own premise:
> Good, there go mine in company with yours!
> And now what are we? unbelievers both,
> Calm and complete, determinately fixed
> To-day, to-morrow and for ever, pray?
> You'll guarantee me that? Not so, I think!
> In no wise! all we've gained is, that belief,
> As unbelief before, shakes us by fits,
> Confounds us like its predecessor. Where's
> The gain? how can we guard our unbelief,
> Make it bear fruit to us? – the problem here.
> Just when we are safest, there's a sunset-touch,
> A fancy from a flower-bell, some one's death,
> A chorus-ending from Euripides, –
> And that's enough for fifty hopes and fears
> As old and new at once as nature's self,
> To rap and knock and enter in our soul,
> Take hands and dance there, a fantastic ring,
> Round the ancient idol, on his base again, –
> The grand Perhaps! We look on helplessly.
> There the old misgivings, crooked questions are –
> This good God, – what he could do, if he would,
> Would, if he could – then must have done long since:
> If so, when, and how? some way must be,

Once feel about, and soon or late you hit
Some sense, in which it might be, after all.
Why not, 'The Way, the Truth, the Life?'

What matter though I doubt at every pore,
Head-doubts, doubts at my fingers' ends,
Doubt in the trivial work of every day,
Doubts at the very bases of my soul
In the grand moments when she probes herself –
If finally I have a life to show,
The thing I did, brought out in evidence
Against the thing done to me underground
By hell and all its brood, for aught I know?
I say, whence sprang this? shows it faith or doubt?
All's doubt in me; where's the break of faith in this?
It is the idea, the feeling and the love,
God means mankind should strive for and show forth
Whatever be the process to that end, –
And not historic knowledge, logic sound,
And metaphysical acumen, sure!
'What think ye of Christ,' friend? when all's done and said,
Like you this Christianity or not?
It may be false, but will you wish it true?
Has it your vote to be so if it can?
Trust you an instinct silenced long ago
That will break silence and enjoin you love
What mortified philosophy is hoarse,
And all in vain, with bidding you despise?
If you desire faith – then you've faith enough.

Pure faith indeed – you know not what you ask!
Naked belief in God the Omnipotent,
Omniscient, Omnipresent, sears too much
The sense of conscious creatures to be borne.
It were the seeing him, no flesh shall dare.
Some think, Creation's meant to show him forth:
I say it's meant to hide him all it can,
And that's what all the blessed evil's for.
Its use in Time is to environ us
Our breath, our drop of dew, with shield enough

179

Against that sight till we can bear its stress.
Under a vertical sun, the exposed brain
And lidless eye and disemprisoned heart
Less certainly would wither up at once
Than mind, confronted with the truth of him.
But time and earth case-harden us to live;
The feeblest sense is trusted most, the child
Feels God a moment, ichors o'er the place,
Plays on and grows to be a man like us.
With me, faith means perpetual unbelief
Kept quiet like the snake 'neath Michael's foot
Who stands calm just because he feels it writhe.
Or if that's too ambitious, – here's my box –
I need the excitation of a pinch
Threatening the torpor of the inside-nose
Nigh on the imminent sneeze that never comes.
'Leave it in peace' advise the simple folk:
Make it aware of peace by itching fits,
Say I – let doubt occasion still more faith!

from *'Christmas Eve and Easter Day'*

. . . God, whose pleasure brought
Man into being, stands away
    As it were a handbreath off, to give
    Room for the newly-made to live,
And look at him from a place apart,
And use his gifts of brain and heart,
Given, indeed, but to keep for ever.
Who speaks of man, then, must not sever
Man's very elements from man,
Saying, 'But all is God's' – whose plan
Was to create man and then leave him
Able, his own word saith, to grieve him,
But able to glorify him too,
As a mere machine could never do,
That prayed or praised, all unaware
Of its fitness for aught but praise and prayer,
Made perfect as a thing of course . . .

from *'Pippa Passes'*

The year's at the spring,
And day's at the morn;
Morning's at seven;
The hill-side's dew-pearled;
The lark's on the wing;
The snail's on the thorn:
God's in his heaven –
All's right with the world!

Frederick William Faber
1814–1863

F. W. Faber had been vicar of Elton in Huntingdonshire for three years when, under Newman's influence, he joined the Roman Catholic Church. After a brief flirtation with his own religious community called 'The Wilfridians' (he was 'Brother Wilfrid') he was asked by Newman to set up the Brompton Oratory in London. His once-famous hymns are too 'Victorian' for modern tastes, but his prose remains popular.

A New Fashion of an Old Sin

Life is short, and it is wearing fast away. We lose a great deal of time, and we want short roads to heaven, though the right road is in truth far shorter than we believe.

What It Is to Have a Creator

We must not only worship God always, but the whole of us must worship God. Our very distractions must be worship, and we must have some kind of worship which will enable them so to be.

Why God Wishes Us to Love Him

A child's first sight of the ocean is an era in his life. It is a new world without him, and it awakens a new world within him. There is no other novelty to be compared with it, and after-life will bring nothing at all like it. A rapid multitude of questions rush upon the mind; yet the child is silent, as if he needed not an answer to any of them. They are beyond answering; and he feels that the sight itself satisfies him better than any answer. Those great bright outspread waters! the idea of God is the only echo to them in his mind: and now henceforth he is a different child because he has seen the sea.

So is it with us when we sit by the ocean of creative love. To gaze – to gaze is all we desire. The fact that so much is mystery to us is no trouble. It is love. That is enough. We trust it. We would almost rather it was not made plainer. It might be darker if it were. Whereas now, though it is indistinct, it is tranquillizing also, like the beauty of a summer night. We have thoughts which cannot be put into words, but it seems to us as if they more than answered all difficulties. How the broad waters flow and shine, and how the many-headed waves leap up to the sun and sparkle, and then sink down into the depths again, yet not to rest; and placid as the azure expanse appears, how evermore it thunders on the hard white sand, and fringes the coast with a bewitching silver mist! Why should we ever stir from where we are?

But when we cease to be children and to be childlike, there is no more this simple enjoyment. We ask questions, not because we doubt, but because when love is not all in all to us, we must have knowledge, or we chafe and pine.

We shall be children once again, and on the same shore, and we shall then never leave it more, and we shall see down into the crystal depths of this creative love, and its wide waters will be the breadth and measure of our joy, and its glancing splendour will be the light of our eternal life, and its soft thunder will be the endless, solemn, thrilling music of our beatitude. Oh happy we! but we must be changed first of all, and perchance by fire!

The Creator and the Creature

Frederick W. Robertson
1816–1853

F. W. Robertson belonged to an unusual breed – a vehement, passionate Broad Churchman, inviting suspicion from both the High Church and the Evangelicals, which latter group he had left because of its intolerance at that time. He was a popular preacher in his day, but his printed sermons had much greater influence after his death.

The Illusiveness of Life

To a child the rainbow is a real thing – substantial and palpable; its limb rests on the side of yonder hill; he believes that he can appropriate it to himself; and when, instead of gems and gold, hid in its radiant bow, he finds nothing but damp mist – cold, dreary drops of disappointment – that disappointment tells that his belief has been delusion.

To the educated man that bow is a blessed illusion, yet it never once deceives; he does not take it for what it is not, he does not expect to make it his own; he feels its beauty as much as the child could feel it, nay infinitely more – more even from the fact that he knows that it will be transient; but besides and beyond this, to him it presents a deeper loveliness; he knows the laws of light, and the laws of the human soul which gave it being. He has linked it with the laws of the universe, and with the invisible mind of God; and it brings to him a thrill of awe, and the sense of a mysterious, nameless beauty, of which the child did not conceive. It is illusion still; but it has fulfilled the promise . . .

God's promises are true, though illusive; far truer than we at first take them to be. We work for a mean, low, sensual happiness, all the while he is leading us on to a spiritual blessedness – unfathomably deep. This is the life of faith. We live by faith, and not by sight.

Christian Progress by Oblivion of the Past

The child that speaks truth for the sake of the praise of truth, is not truthful. The man who is honest because honesty is the best policy, has not integrity in his heart. He who endeavours to be humble, and holy, and perfect, in order to win heaven, has only a counterfeit religion. God for His own sake – Goodness because it is good – Truth because it is lovely – this is the Christian's aim. The prize is only an incentive: inseparable from success, but not the aim itself.

Religious Depression

Mourning after an absent God is an evidence of love as strong as rejoicing in a present one. Nay further, a man may be more decisively the servant of God and goodness while doubting His existence, and in the anguish of his soul crying for light, than while resting in a common creed, and coldly serving Him. There has been one at least whose apparent forsakenness, and whose seeming doubt, bears the stamp of the majesty of Faith. 'My God, my God, why hast thou forsaken me?' . . .

There are times when a dense cloud veils the sunlight: you cannot see the sun, nor feel him. Sensitive temperaments feel depression: and that unaccountably and irresistibly. No effort can make you *feel*. Then you hope. Behind the cloud the sun is: from thence he will come: the day drags through, the darkest and longest night ends at last. Thus we bear the darkness and the otherwise intolerable cold, and many a sleepless night. It does not shine now – but it will. So too, spiritually.

There are hours in which physical derangement darkens the windows of the soul; days in which shattered nerves make life simply endurance; months and years in which intellectual difficulties, pressing for solution, shut out God. Then faith must be replaced by hope . . .

The mistake we make is to look for a source of comfort in ourselves: self-contemplation instead of gazing upon God. In other words, we look for comfort precisely where comfort never can be.

For it is impossible to derive consolation from our own feelings, because of their mutability: to-day we are well, and our spiritual experience, partaking of these circumstances, is bright: but to-morrow some outward circumstances change – the sun does not shine, or the wind is chill, and we are low, gloomy, and sad. Then, if our hopes were unreasonably elevated, they will now be unreasonably depressed; and so our experience becomes flux and reflux, ebb and flow; like the sea, that emblem of instability . . .

God is not affected by our mutability: our changes do not alter Him. When we are restless, He remains serene and calm: when we are low, selfish, mean, or dispirited, He is still the unalterable I AM. The same yesterday, today, and for ever, in whom is no variableness, neither shadow of turning. What God is in Himself, not what we may chance to feel Him in this or that moment to be, that is our hope. 'My soul, hope thou *in God.*'

The Power of Sorrow

To grieve over sin is one thing, to repent of it is another . . .

Sorrow has two results; it may end in spiritual life, or in spiritual death; and, in themselves, one of these is as natural as the other. Sorrow may produce two kinds of reformation – a transient, or a permanent one – an alteration in habits, which, originating in emotion, will last so long as that emotion continues, and then, after a few fruitless efforts, be given up – a repentance which will be repented of; or, again, a permanent change, which will be reversed by no after thought – a repentance not to be repented of. Sorrow is, in itself, therefore, a thing neither good nor bad; its value depends on the spirit of the person on whom it falls. Fire will inflame straw, soften iron, or harden clay; its effects are determined by the object with which it comes in contact . . . So too with sorrow. There are spirits in which it develops the seminal principle of life; there are others in which it prematurely hastens the consummation of irreparable decay . . .

The religion which is only sunned into being by happiness, is a suspicious thing: having been warmed by joy, it will become cold when joy is over; and then, when these blessings are removed, we count ourselves hardly treated, as if we had been defrauded of a right.

Sermons on Religion and Life

Christina Rossetti
1830–1894

Christina Rossetti, one of England's foremost women poets, was a devout member of the Church of England and rejected two offers of marriage as unsuitable on religious grounds: one suitor was an agnostic, the other a Roman Catholic. Her devotional poetry and prose has spiritual longing as its recurring theme.

After Communion

Why should I call Thee Lord, Who art my God?
    Why should I call Thee Friend, Who art my Love?
Or King, Who art my very Spouse above?
Or call Thy Sceptre on my heart Thy rod?
    Lo now Thy banner over me is love,
All heaven flies open to me at Thy nod:
For Thou hast lit Thy flame in me a clod,
    Made me a nest for dwelling of Thy Dove.
    What wilt Thou call me in our home above,
Who now hast called me friend? how will it be
    When Thou for good wine settest forth the best?
Now Thou dost bid me come and sup with Thee,
    Now Thou dost make me lean upon Thy breast:
How will it be with me in time of love?

Lord, Purge Our Eyes to See

Lord, purge our eyes to see
Within the seed a tree,
Within the glowing egg a bird,
Within the shroud a butterfly.
Till, taught by such we see
Beyond all creatures, Thee.

O Lord Seek Us, O Lord Find Us

O Lord seek us, O Lord find us
In Thy patient care,
Be Thy love before, behind us,
Round us everywhere.

Lest the god of this world blind us,
Lest he bait a snare,
Lest he forge a chain to bind us,
Lest he speak us fair,
Turn not from us, call to mind us,
Find, embrace us, hear.
Be Thy love before, behind us,
Round us everywhere.

O my God, bestow upon us such confidence, such peace, such happiness in Thee, that Thy will may always be dearer to us than our own will, and Thy pleasure than our own pleasure. All that Thou givest is Thy free gift to us, all that Thou takest away Thy grace to us. Be Thou thanked for all, praised for all, loved for all; through Jesus Christ our Lord.

O Lord, shield of our help, who wilt not suffer us to be tempted above that we are able, help us, we entreat thee, in all our straits and wrestlings, to lift up our eyes unto thee, and stay our hearts on thee, through Jesus Christ.

Lord Jesus, so long as seemeth Thee good, give us faith rather than knowledge, and hope rather than assurance. Feed us when we need feeding; heal us when we need healing. Grant us to find peace by conforming ourselves lovingly to Thy goodwill and pleasure – peace here and peace hereafter; through Jesus Christ our Lord.

Prayers

Gerard Manley Hopkins
1844–1889

Hopkins always felt that his poetic talent was at odds with his calling as a Jesuit priest. At one point he laid up his pen for seven years, and later asked his friend Robert Bridges to destroy his work upon his death. Bridges' disobedience saved for us some of the most brilliantly compact expressions of God's immanence in his creation.

The Windhover

I caught this morning morning's minion, king-
    dom of daylight's dauphin, dapple-dawn-drawn Falcon,
      in his riding
    Of the rolling level underneath him steady air, and
      striding
High there, how he rung upon the rein of a wimpling wing
In his ecstasy! then off, off forth on swing,
    As a skate's heel sweeps smooth on a bow-bend: the
      hurl and gliding
    Rebuffed the big wind. My heart in hiding
Stirred for a bird, – the achieve of, the mastery of the thing!

Brute beauty and valour and act, oh, air, pride, plume, here
    Buckle! AND the fire that breaks from thee then, a billion
Times told lovelier, more dangerous, O my chevalier!

    No wonder of it, shéer plód makes plough down sillion
Shine, and blue-bleak embers, ah my dear,
    Fall, gall themselves, and gash gold-vermilion.

'Thou Art Indeed Just'

*Justus quidem tu es, Domine, si disputem tecum; verumtamen
justa loquar ad te: Quare via impiorum prosperatur? etc.*

Thou art indeed just, Lord, if I contend
With thee; but, sir, so what I plead is just.
Why do sinners' ways prosper? and why must
Disappointment all I endeavour end?

Wert thou my enemy, O thou my friend,
How wouldst thou worse, I wonder, than thou dost
Defeat, thwart me? Oh, the sots and thralls of lust
Do in spare hours more thrive than I that spend,

Sir, life upon thy cause. See, banks and brakes
Now, leavèd how thick! lacèd they are again
With fretty chervil, look, and fresh wind shakes

Them; birds build—but not I build; no, but strain,
Time's eunuch, and not breed one work that wakes.
Mine, O thou lord of life, send my roots rain.

Our Lord Jesus Christ, my brethren, is our hero, a hero all the world wants. You know how books of tales are written, that put one man before the reader and shew him off handsome for the most part and brave and call him My Hero or Our Hero.

Often mothers make a hero of a son; girls of a sweetheart and good wives of a husband. Soldiers make a hero of a great general, a party of its leader, a nation of any great man that brings it glory, whether king, warrior, statesman, thinker, poet, or whatever it shall be.

But Christ, he is the hero. He too is the hero of a book or books, of the divine gospels. He is a warrior and a conqueror; of whom it is written he went forth conquering and to conquer. He is a king, Jesus of Nazareth king of the Jews, though when he came to his own kingdom his own did not receive him, and now, his people having cast him off, we Gentiles are his inheritance. He is a statesman, that drew up the New Testament in his blood and founded the Roman Catholic Church that cannot fail. He is a thinker, that taught us divine mysteries. He is an orator and poet, as in his eloquent words and parables appears. He is all the world's hero, the desire of nations.

But besides he is the hero of single souls; his mother's hero, not out of motherly foolish fondness but because he was, as the angel told her, great and the son of the Most High and all that he did and said and was done and said about him she laid up in her heart. He is the truelove and the bridegroom of men's souls; the virgins follow him whithersoever he goes; the martyrs follow him through a sea of blood, through great tribulation; all his servants take up their cross and follow him. And those even that do not follow him, yet they look wistfully after him, own him a hero, and wish they dared answer to his call.

– from a sermon preached on Sunday evening, 23 November 1879 at Bedford Leigh (Luke 2:33 *Et erat pater ejus et mater mirantes super his quae dicebantur de illo*).

. . . When a man is in God's grace and free from mortal sin, then everything that he does, so long as there is no sin in it, gives God glory and what does not give him glory has some, however little, sin in it. It is not only prayer that gives God glory but work. Smiting on an anvil, sawing a beam, white-washing a wall, driving horses, sweeping, scouring, everything gives God some glory if being in his grace you do it as your duty. To go to communion worthily gives God great glory, but to take food in thankfulness and temperance gives him glory too. To lift up the hands in prayer gives God glory, but a man with a dungfork in his hand, a woman with a sloppail, give him glory too. He is so great that all things give him glory if you mean they should. So then, my brethren, live.

> The conclusion of 'The Principle or Foundation', an address based on the opening of *The Spiritual Exercises* of St Ignatius Loyola.

Friedrich von Hügel
1852–1925

The son of an Austrian diplomat, Friedrich von Hügel was brought to England as a teenager. He was a devout Roman Catholic, but came under suspicion for his 'modernist' theological views. He kept up over six years a correspondence with his niece Gwendolen, to whom he gave much practical spiritual advice, often couched in powerful images, and with whom he shared his own inner experiences.

The material of the Supernatural is not only the heroic but also, indeed mostly, the homely.

Let me give you three images, all of which have helped me on along 'many a flinty furlong'. At eighteen I learnt from Father Raymond Hecking, that grandly interior-minded Dominican, that I certainly could, with God's grace, give myself to him, and strive to live my life long with him and for him. But that this would mean winning and practising much desolation – that I would be climbing a mountain where, off and on, I might be enveloped in mist for days on end, unable to see a foot before me. Had I noticed how mountaineers climb mountains? how they have a quiet, regular, short step – on the level it looks petty; but then this step they keep up, on and on, as they ascend, whilst the inexperienced townsman hurries along, and soon has to stop, dead beat with the climb. That such an expert mountaineer, when the thick mists come, halts and camps out under some slight cover brought with him, quietly smoking his pipe, and moving on only when the mist has cleared away.

Then in my thirties I utilised another image, learnt in my Jesuit Retreats. How I was taking a long journey on board ship, with great storms pretty sure ahead of me; and how I must now select, and fix in my little cabin, some few but entirely appropriate things – a small trunk fixed up at one end, a chair that would keep its position, tumbler and glass that would do ditto: all this, simple, strong, and selected throughout in view of stormy weather. So would my spirituality have to be chosen and cultivated especially in view of 'dirty' weather.

And lastly, in my forties another image helped me – they all three are in pretty frequent use still! I am travelling on a camel across a huge desert. Windless days occur, and then all is well. But hurricanes of wind will come, unforeseen, tremendous. What to do then? It is very simple, but it takes much practice to do well at all. Dismount from the camel, fall prostrate face downwards on the sand, covering your head with your cloak. And lie thus, an hour, three hours, half a day: the sand storm will go, and you will arise, and continue your journey as if nothing had happened. The old Uncle has had many, many such sand storms. How immensely useful they are!

You see, whether it be great cloud-mists on the mountain-side, or huge, mountain-high waves on the ocean, or blinding sand storms in the desert: there is each time one crucial point – to form no conclusions, to take no decisions, to change nothing during such crises, and especially at such times, not to force any particularly religious mood or idea in oneself. To turn gently to other things, to maintain a vague, general attitude of resignation – to be very meek, with oneself and with others: the crisis goes by, thus, with great fruit.

Child of my old Heart . . .
The wise way to fight antipathies is never to fight them

191

directly – turn gently to other sights, images, thoughts, etc. If it – the hate – persists, bear it gently like a fever or a toothache – do not speak to it – better not speak of it even to God. But gently turn to Him your love and life, and tell Him gently that you want Him and all of Him: and that you beg for courage whilst He thus leaves you dressed, or seeing yourself dressed, in what you do not want to endorse as a will decision, but only as purgation if so He wills. It is an itch – scratching makes it worse. Away out into God's great world – even if your immediate landscape is just your unlovely antipathies.

Pray for your Uncle to become very, very humble – to disappear from one's own sight – with just God and souls; and one's little self one of these souls; how glorious that would be . . .

Loving old Uncle,
H

I wait for the breath of God, for God's breath. Perhaps he will call me to-day – to-night. Don't let us be niggardly towards God. He is never a niggard towards us. Let us try to be generous and accept. My illness is so little! I have no pain – my brain is clear – why should I not accept this generously? I would like to finish my book – but if not, I shall live it out in the Beyond. I love the angels, they stand for something we cannot otherwise express . . .

Plant yourself on foundations that are secure – God – Christ – Suffering – the Cross. They are secure. How I love the Sacraments! I am as certain of the real presence of Christ in the Eucharist as of anything there is. Our great hope is in Christianity – our only hope. Christ re-creates. Christianity has taught us to care. Caring is the greatest thing – caring matters most. My faith is not enough – it comes and goes. I have it about some things and not about others. So we make up and supplement each other. We give and others give to us. Keep your life a life of prayer, dearie. Keep it like that; it's the only thing, and remember, no joy without suffering – no patience without trial – no humility without humiliation – no life without death.

Letters to a Niece

John Chapman
1865–1933

Dom John Chapman is now best remembered as a spiritual adviser, though he was also an able biblical scholar and linguist. He learnt his central message of patience and submission to God during a life which involved many changes of direction. He was first an Anglican curate, then a Roman Catholic, tried the Jesuits, became a Benedictine and then served in various places in Western Europe, ending up abbot of Downside Abbey.

[Undated]

A 'state of prayer' lasts an hour, or five minutes, as the case may be, but it is seldom habitual, for people vary at different hours of the day. We cannot choose, but have to do our best, and take what God sends us. It is right, I think, to feel perfectly satisfied (after our prayer) that it *is* all right when it *feels* all wrong. We humble ourselves and say: 'O God, I cannot pray. I cannot even keep in Thy presence.' Or, 'I cannot pray as I did yesterday; but I only want to do Thy Will, not to be satisfied with my prayer.'

It is of the very essence of prayer that it does not depend on us. It depends on circumstances – our stomach, our preoccupations, much more than on our will – for the character it takes; and, naturally, on God's special grace. But possibly the *best* kind is when we seem unable to do anything, if then we throw ourselves on God, and stay contentedly before Him; worried, anxious, tired, listless, but – above all and under it all – humbled and abandoned to His will, contented with our own discontent.

If we can get ourselves accustomed to this attitude of soul, which is always possible, we have learned how to pray.

August 29, 1916

If you are drawn to contemplative prayer, you are also drawn to a passive form of spirituality, in which God does all, while we wait and wonder. Consequently, give yourself to prayer, when you can, and trust in God that He will lead you, without

193

your choosing your path. Mr Asquith is an excellent model (not for Cabinet Ministers, but) for contemplatives: wait for pressure from without; do not act unless you must; let the Daily Mail take the initiative.

Be sure that if you give yourself up blindly to God's Will, all will come right, though it may seem all wrong. Do not worry, but be confident. If you cannot pray in the least, and only waste time, and moon, and wander, still hold on; on no account ever make a violent decision.

February 16, 1918

You are the block, God is the sculptor; you cannot know what He is hitting you for, and you *never will* in this life. All you want is patience, trust, confidence, and He does it all. It is very simple – simplicity itself.

January 20, 1925

As to your uselessness, that is a good feeling. *We cannot be useful to God!* He can do without us perfectly well. But if He chooses to use us, it is a great honour. Only we do not generally know that He is using us.

July 18, 1914

We *must* have our times of desolation and trial. How can we show our love of God except by enduring? He showed His love for us by suffering . . .

It is a great grace that God should humble us, and give us something to bear for Him. Of course you would like some other trial instead! One always prefers an imaginary trial to an actual one! Humble yourself; don't expect to be devout, or happy either; declare before God that you are incapable of a good thought; and you will find the only peace worth having.

December 19, 1919

The one real proof that you have the *right kind of prayer for you,* is not that it always goes easily and always succeeds, but that it really does you good and changes your life.

October 13, 1925

Lastly – think as little as you can about all this. God is using the surgeon's knife – you cannot help Him by watching it – He could act better if you were distracted by something else! Try to get above yourself; laugh at your own troubles; say you know they will pass.

So they will: for it seems to be a fact that God *always gives breathing-spaces*.

February 16, 1927

For our bodily health we must use ordinary prudence, ordinary food and exercise. But if we are always thinking about it, we become valetudinarians, and are never well! So with our souls – but even more so, for here God is our *Doctor!* He is not only the healthy air in which we live (which cures us more than any medicine): but He gives the medicine in the right doses, and we have only to accept it. Confidence in Him is what we want. Our dryness and distractions are *very* nasty medicines, though.

November 21, 1930

God can lead us as He likes, and will. We ought not to choose, but to be carried in His arms. Of course it is not natural to like being carried. We want to walk and look about.

Spiritual Letters

Evelyn Underhill
1875–1941

Evelyn Underhill is in a direct line from Von Hügel, who became her spiritual director in 1921. She in turn provided guidance to many others, not least in the retreats she led. She was largely responsible for awakening twentieth-century interest in mysticism, both through her own work and by producing translations of Hilton, Rolle and The Cloud of Unknowing.

To love God, without demand or measure, in and for Himself – this is Charity: and Charity is the spiritual life.

Only this most gently powerful of all attractions and all pressures can capture and purify the will of man and subordinate it to the great purpose of God; for as His Love and Will are One, so the love and will of man must become one. Therefore all other purifications, disciplines and practices have meaning because they prepare and contribute to the invasion and transformation of the heart by the uncreated Charity of God. 'Thou art the Love wherewith the heart loves Thee.'

For it is only when the secret thrust of our whole being is thus re-ordered by God and set towards God, that peace is established in the house of life. Then the disorderly energies of emotion and will are rectified and harmonised, and all the various and wide-spreading love which we pour out towards other souls and things is deepened, unselfed and made safe; because that which is now sought and loved in them is the immanent Divine thought and love. Thus the will transformed in Charity everywhere discovers God.

Reason and love combine to assure us that our end is God alone; first realised as an influence, one amongst other claims and objects of desire, and then, as we more and more respond to His attraction, as the only satisfaction of the heart; and at last as the all-penetrating, all-compelling Reality, that only Life which is recognised by Faith, desired in Hope, achieved by Charity. Then all these separate movements of love and longing – those passionate self-givings and agonies of desire – in which the struggling and half-awakened spirit reaches out towards life and draws back to the prison of solitary pain, find their solution and satisfaction in God; and there is established in her that steadfast habitude of love which makes her the open channel and docile instrument of the one Divine Love.

It is the special function of prayer to turn the self away from the time-series and towards the eternal order; away from the apparent and towards the significant; away from succession and towards adoration and adherence. Prayer opens the door of the psyche to the invasion of another order, which shall at its full term transform the very quality of our existence. And

Spirit, in its most general sense, is our name for that world, life, Being, which is then apprehended by us; and for that quality in ourselves which is capable of such apprehension and response . . . We do not mean by it some tenuous region or plane to which physical considerations cannot apply. The whole witness of religion suggests that it is alive with an awful splendour, a range of personal action, which extends from the most tender and intimate workings on the individual soul, to the inconceivable energies and secret movements which can sometimes be detected behind the pageant of the visible world.

There is no correspondence, no parity, between our most admirable notions and the Being of God; and we only begin to approach a certain obscure knowledge of His presence when we consent to abandon our arrogant attempts towards definition and understanding, become the meek recipients of His given lights, and the silent worshippers of His unfathomable Reality. Only by a movement of bare faith does the mind really draw near to Him.

The Golden Sequence

It is not easy to disentangle will and feeling; for in all intense will there is a strong element of emotion – every volitional act has somewhere at the back of it a desire – and in all great and energising passions there is a pronounced volitional element. The 'synthesis of love and will' is no mere fancy of the psychologist. It is a compound hard to break down in practice. But I think we can say generally that the business of feeling is to inflame the will, to give it intention, gladness and vividness; to convert it from a dull determination into an eager, impassioned desire. It links up thought and action.

Love should give two things to prayer: ardour and beauty. In his prayer, as it were, man swings a censer before the altar of the universe. He may put into the thurible all his thoughts and dreams, all his will and energy. But unless the fire of love is communicated to that incense, nothing will happen; there will be no fragrance and no ascending smoke. These qualities – ardour and beauty – represent two distinct types of feeling, which ought both to find a place in the complete spiritual life, balancing and completing one another.

The Essentials of Mysticism

Let us consider this picture which comes to us from the great Biblical poem of the Creation. Darkness, chaos, mystery: and yet, already manifest, the first of all energies and actions, the cherishing, loving action of God. Love that hopes all and does all, brooding on the formless, unpromising deeps.

Beyond the ceaseless movement, the flaming sun, the vast spaces of the material universe, as science shows it to us, the Poet of the Universe, the Creative Spirit of God, brooding, with the patient, fostering action of love, on His restless, unformed, chaotic, empty world. And the author of the passage in Genesis does not see those dark waters, that chaos lashed by spiritual action into great waves.

It is not the dreadful energy and infinite space of the stellar universe which strike him first. He takes us beyond all that and shows us the world as it comes into being under the action of the Thought of God – Brooding. The true majesty of the Creative Action is manifest in its quietness. Bit by bit, the tranquil, brooding Spirit draws forth their latent possibilities, the beauty, wonder, variety of life.

So the great Thinker broods unhurried on His material, as a great musician on a theme, till the moment of creation comes, and life, truth and beauty appear. But really that long, brooding, quiet, when nothing seems to happen – the mind and will intent on that which is to be, when all is still, without form and void – *this* is part and a great part of the action of Creation. Here 'the Holy Ghost over the bent world broods'. Here the Eternal Artist, Eternal Love, is at work.

So we dwell on this great picture of Creation, lying under the warm shadow of His wings: the quietness of the dark waters, those mysterious deeps with all their unrealised possibilities of life, beauty and power – and the patient, loving presence of God, the Perfect, Who, by His ceaseless action on the imperfect, alone gives form and brings forth life. We are not looking on something finished and done with; we look, so far as we dare, at an Eternal process – the increasing actions of the Divine Love.

Meditations and Prayers

William Temple
1881–1944

William Temple followed in his father's footsteps right into Lambeth Palace. His time as Archbishop of Canterbury was marked by a benevolent respect for other people's beliefs. This grew out of his theological view that Christ is responsible for all that is good in all beliefs.

To the religious man every activity is religious. He eats and drinks religiously, of which 'grace' at meals is the symbol; he works religiously, for his work is his life-service to God; he plays religiously, for his recreation is with thanksgiving; but above all he sins religiously. To do wrong is for an irreligious man to abandon his ideal and perhaps to lower his self-respect. For the religious man to do wrong is to defy his King: for the Christian, it is to wound his Friend. It is here that for many people the distinctively religious experience is most acute . . .

Prayer is often regarded, even by genuinely religious people, as chiefly a means to various ends; it is a way of getting things done. That is true, so far as it goes; but, like so many half-truths, it is in practice as misleading as a complete falsehood. Prayer which is mainly occupied with a result to be obtained is comparatively powerless to obtain results. The real significance of prayer lies in the fact that it is the effort and attitude of the soul which makes possible the unity of the human spirit with God; it is therefore itself the supreme aim of human existence . . .

The proper relation in thought between prayer and conduct is not that conduct is supremely important and prayer may help it, but that prayer is supremely important and conduct tests it. If the prayer is real, the conduct inevitably follows. Indeed, in many cases the very reality of prayer will shorten the time allotted to prayer, so strong will be the impulse of love to act for the well-being of others. But let any man who finds it thus with him take heed. The life with God is the supreme concern, and the source of all power to serve. It is only the man who loves God with all his being who will be able to love his neighbour as himself.

Christus Veritas

Rose Macaulay
1881–1958

A prolific essayist, novelist and broadcaster, Rose Macaulay rediscovered her Anglican faith late in life through a correspondence with a Cowley Father, Fr Johnson (published as Letters to a Friend*). Her religious search, and her love for a married man which had made it difficult, were the subjects of her last novel,* The Towers of Trebizond.

28th January 1951

. . . I like it so much [Fr Johnson's previous letter]; particularly the bit about being inside the house, and the growth possible there – the gradual appreciation of one's inheritance. That comes home to me just now.

I told you once that I couldn't *really* regret the past. But now I do regret it, very much. It's as if absolution and communion and prayer let us through into a place where we get a horribly clear view – a new view – so that we see all the waste, and the cost of it, and how its roots struck deep down into the earth, poisoning the springs of our own lives and other people's. Such waste, such cost in human and spiritual values. The priest says, 'Go in peace, the Lord has put away thy sin.' But of course one doesn't go in peace, and in one sense He can't put it away, it has done its work. You can't undo what's done . . . It's not a question of forgiveness, but of irrevocable damage done.

Perhaps I shall mind more and more, all my life. Is this what absolution and communion do to one? I see now why belief in God fades away and has to go, while one is leading a life one knows to be wrong. The two can't live together. It doesn't give even intellectual acceptance a chance. Now it *has* its chance. I don't, you know, attach much importance to *details* of belief – I don't feel they really matter (or do they?). But I hold on to your remark – 'we may be sure that at the bottom of the whole business there is a personal relationship,' which is possibly all that matters. After what has occurred to me lately, I *know* there is . . .

Letters to a Friend

I was getting into a stage when I was not quite sure what sin was, I was in a kind of fog, drifting about without clues, and this is liable to happen when you go on and on doing something, it makes a confused sort of twilight in which everything is blurred, and the next thing you know you might be stealing or anything, because right and wrong have become things you do not look at, you are afraid to, and it seems better to live in a blur. Then come the times when you wake suddenly up, and the fog breaks, and right and wrong loom through it, sharp and clear like peaks of a rock, and you are on the wrong peak and know that, unless you can manage to leave it now, you may be marooned there for life and ever after. Then, as you don't leave it, the mist swirls round again, and hides the other peak, and you turn your back on it and try to forget it and succeed.

Another thing you learn about sin, it is not one deed more than another, though the Church may call some of them mortal and others not, but even the worst ones are only the result of one choice after another and part of a chain, not things by themselves . . . And while I am on sin, I have often thought that it is a most strange thing that this important part of human life, the struggle that almost every one has about good and evil, cannot now be talked of without embarrassment, unless of course one is in church . . .

Once people used to talk about being good and being bad, they wrote about it in letters to their friends, and conversed about it freely; the Greeks did this, and the Romans, and then, after life took a Christian turn, people did it more than ever, and all throughout the Middle Ages they did it, and throughout the Renaissance, and drama was full of it, and heaven and hell seemed for ever round the corner, with people struggling on the borderlines and never knowing which way it was going to turn out, and in which of these two states they would be spending their immortality, and this led to a lot of conversation about it all, and it was extremely interesting and exciting . . .

I am not sure when all this died out, but it has now become very dead. I do not remember that when I was at Cambridge we talked much about such things, they were thought rather CICCU and shunned, though we talked about

201

everything else, such as religion, love, people, psychoanalysis, books, art, places, cooking, cars, food, sex, and all that. And still we talk about all these other things, but not about being good or bad. You can say you would like to be a good writer, or painter, or architect, or swimmer, or carpenter, or cook, or actor, or climber, or talker, or even, I suppose, a good husband or wife, but not that you would like to be a good person, which is a desire you can only mention to a clergyman, whose shop it is, and who must not object or make dry answers like an unbribed oracle, but must listen and try to assist you in your vain ambition.

The Towers of Trebizond

Virginia Woolf
1882–1941

Virginia Woolf's novels and literary criticism have greatly influenced twentieth-century literature, her fluid style reflecting the blurred edge between truth and sensation. She suffered from periodic bouts of acute depression, eventually committing suicide when she felt another coming upon her.

I have some restless searcher in me. Why is there not a discovery in life? Something one can lay hands on and say 'This is it'? My depression is a harassed feeling. I'm looking: but that's not it – that's not it. What is it? And shall I die before I find it? Then (as I was walking through Russell Square last night) I see the mountains in the sky: the great clouds; and the moon which is risen over Persia; I have a great and astonishing sense of something there, which is 'it'. It is not exactly beauty that I mean. It is that the thing is in itself enough: satisfactory; achieved. A sense of my own strangeness, walking on the earth is there too: of the infinite oddity of the human position; trotting along Russell Square with the moon up there and those mountain clouds. Who am I, what am I, and so on: these questions are always floating about in me: and then I bump against some exact fact – a letter, a person, and come to them again with a great sense of freshness. And so it goes on. But on this showing, which is true, I think, I do fairly frequently come upon this 'it'; and then feel quite at rest.

A Writer's Diary

Catherine Bramwell-Booth
b. 1883

The grandchildren of William Booth, the founder of the Salvation Army, Catherine and her six brothers and sisters all followed their parents into what their father called 'the Concern'. Catherine's active service has lasted past her 100th birthday, when she became a rather bemused media personality. In her late twenties Catherine found she was getting a number of letters asking for advice from ex-cadets whom she had taught. Her father suggested she reply to them in the Army's magazine and these replies were eventually published as a book.

May 1916

My Dear G—,

I was reminded of you the other evening by a scrubbing brush and a tambourine – both ancient and both retired from active service. Not that I mean to imply that you are! Far from it. Still, I was reminded of you, and so I am writing.

Do you remember the two articles in question? They now decorate the wall of my room at the Lodge . . . They remind me how really splendid it was to be a cadet, and to have enjoyed being one, and how still more wonderfully joyful to have had, and still to have, a chance of going ahead with the work.

When I look at the scrubber, the actual companion of the first duties that entering the work entailed, I am glad it means to me now, as it meant then, the work of the hands as well as of the heart and mind. 'Body, soul, and spirit, Jesus, I give to Thee.'

If I were ever in danger of getting above scrubology, I hope the sight of the old original would make me ashamed. Just now I often wish there were more opportunity for that kind of service, but the wish is rather a lazy one. It has always been an easier thing to me to serve others in *doing* something

203

for them than by merely talking to them, especially when they seldom really want to hear what you have to say . . . However, whether I have many chances or few the old brush tells me to take them, to see to it that I live up to the old ideal of anything and everything as a love service to souls and bodies for Jesus' sake. It tells me also that it is the spirit that sanctifies the work, as it truly did when I scrubbed the dining room in those dear old Training College days. So now we can – I can – you can do all in the spirit of the Lord Jesus. Isn't it wonderful to realise it?

The tambourine joins in all the time, and particularly emphasises that I must be cheerful and courageous. When I first used it I was a fearing, feeble creature. The tambourine often helped me to hide that fact, and perhaps I began to learn what it meant to offer the sacrifice of praise in those first days of playing – how to praise when it would have been easier to grumble! The cheerful sound of jingles is symbolical of that brave spirit that helps me to smile in the face of failure – anyway in face of aggravations.

I wish I had a more naturally smiling face and a less worrying spirit; because I do believe in the 'Happy Sally' religion. That's one of the things that the tambourine stands for to me – so I still play one, as well as listen respectfully to what my pensioned one says . . .

Anyway, there they are on the wall, the brush and the timbrel – worn out, valueless; and one day they will land on the dust heap either by accident or design. But I do pray that, for me, while I live, the gospel of each day may be a part of my religion. To serve, and to serve with joy; not only inside joy, but joy expressed in such a fashion as others may know my work *is* a joy – courage to rejoice in hope even when I cannot in fact, and love to serve even in the lowest, with such a spirit as shall raise it to the highest.

It is ages since I heard from you, and longer still since I saw you; but I should like to see you, and feel sure that you would not feel awkward with either a scrubber or a tambourine – whichever circumstances demanded. I can truthfully say I should not.

Yours, serving with joy . . .

Letters

Geoffrey Studdert-Kennedy
1883–1929

Studdert-Kennedy earned his more famous nickname, 'Woodbine Willie', from his time as an army chaplain during World War I when he would carry a rucksack of cigarettes to hand out to the troops at the front. The experience only served to strengthen his love of the working classes which had started during his childhood in a tough Leeds slum.

Close by the Heedless Worker's Side

Close by the heedless worker's side,
    Still patient stands
The carpenter of Nazareth,
    With pierced hands
Outstretched to plead unceasingly
    His love's demands;

Longing to pick the hammer up
    And strike a blow;
Longing to feel his plane swing out,
    Steady and slow,
The fragrant shavings falling down
    Silent as snow.

Because this is my work, O Lord,
    It must be thine;
Because it is a human task
    It is divine.
Take me, and brand me with thy Cross,
    Thy slave's proud sign.

When Through the Whirl of Wheels

When through the whirl of wheels, and engines humming,
    Patiently powerful for the sons of men,
Peals like a trumpet promise of his coming
    Who in the clouds is pledged to come again;

When through the night the furnace fires a-flaring,
    Shooting out tongues of flame like leaping blood,

Speak to the heart of Love, alive and daring,
  Sing of the boundless energy of God;

When in the depths the patient miner striving
  Feels in his arms and vigour of the Lord,
Strikes for a kingdom and his King's arriving,
  Holding his pick more splendid than the sword;

When on the sweat of labour and its sorrow,
  Toiling in twilight flickering and dim,
Flames out the sunshine of the great to-morrow,
  When all the world looks up because of him –

Then will he come with meekness for his glory,
  God in a workman's jacket as before,
Living again the eternal gospel story,
  Sweeping the shavings from his workshop floor.

The Unutterable Beauty

Anna Bunston
?

*We have tried to find out something – anything – about Anna Bunston
. . . but have failed. All we know is that when she married she became
Mrs Bunston de Bary and that her* Collected Poems *appeared in
1947; all a bit untidy but we like the poem too much to leave it out.*

Under a Wiltshire Apple Tree

Some folk as can afford,
So I've heard say,
Set up a sort of cross
Right in the garden way
To mind 'em of the Lord.

But I, when I do see
Thik apple tree
An' stoopin' limb
All spread wi' moss,
I think of Him
And how He talks wi' me.

I think of God
And how He trod
That garden long ago;
He walked, I reckon, to and fro
And then sat down
Upon the groun'
Or some low limb
What suited Him
Such as you see
On many a tree,
And on thik very one
Where I at set o' sun
Do sit and talk wi' He.

And, mornings too, I rise and come
An' sit down where the branch be low;
And bird do sing, a bee do hum,
The flowers in the border blow,
And all my heart's so glad and clear
As pools when mists do disappear:
As pools a-laughing in the light
When mornin' air is swep' an' bright,
As pools what got all Heaven in sight
So's my heart's cheer
When He be near.

He never pushed the garden door,
He left no footmark on the floor;
I never heard 'Un stir nor tread
And yet His Hand do bless my head,
And when 'tis time for work to start
I takes Him with me in my heart.

And when I die, pray God I see
At very last thik apple tree
An' stoopin' limb,
And think of Him
And all He been to me.

D. H. Lawrence
1885–1930

Not primarily known as a religious writer, Lawrence nevertheless continued to be drawn to spiritual and mystical themes. His last book, for instance, was a personal examination of the Book of Revelation.

Pax

All that matters is to be at one with the living God
to be a creature in the house of the God of Life.

Like a cat asleep on a chair
at peace, in peace
and at one with the master of the house, with the mistress,
at home, at home in the house of the living,
sleeping on the hearth, and yawning before the fire.

Sleeping on the hearth of the living world
yawning at home before the fire of life
feeling the presence of the living God
like a great reassurance
a deep calm in the heart
a presence
as of a master sitting at the board
in his own and greater being,
in the house of life.

When the wonder has gone out of a man he is dead. When all comes to all, the most precious element in life is wonder. Love is a great emotion and power is power. But both love and power are based on wonder. Plant consciousness, insect consciousness, fish consciousness, animal consciousness, all are related by one permanent element, which we may call the religious element in all life, even in a flea: the sense of wonder. That is our sixth sense. And it is the *natural* religious sense.

The Phoenix

Somehow I think we come into knowledge (unconscious) of the most vital parts of the cosmos through touching things.

Such a touch is the connection between the vigorous flow of
two lives. Like a positive electricity, a current of creative life
runs through two persons and they are instinctive with the
same life-force.

Letters

T. S. Eliot
1888–1965

*Although born in Missouri, Eliot became a British citizen in 1927,
declaring himself to be 'classical in literature, royalist in politics
and Anglo-Catholic in religion'. Four Quartets is the clearest
expression of his spiritual exploration and the height of his literary
achievement. His attachment to Little Gidding was a lasting one and
in 1947 he helped found the 'Friends of Little Gidding'.*

from *'East Coker'*

Home is where one starts from. As we grow older
The world becomes stranger, the pattern more complicated
Of dead and living. Not the intense moment
Isolated, with no before and after,
But a lifetime burning in every moment
And not the lifetime of one man only
But of old stones that cannot be deciphered.
There is a time for the evening under starlight,
A time for the evening under lamplight
(The evening with the photograph album).
Love is most nearly itself
When here and now cease to matter.

from *'Little Gidding'*

        . . . If you came this way,
Taking the route you would be likely to take
From the place you would be likely to come from,
If you came this way in may time, you would find the hedges
White again, in May, with voluptuary sweetness.
It would be the same at the end of the journey,

If you came at night like a broken king,
If you came by day not knowing what you came for,
It would be the same, when you leave the rough road
And turn behind the pig-sty to the dull façade
And the tombstone. And what you thought you came for
Is only a shell, a husk of meaning
From which the purpose breaks only when it is fulfilled
If at all. Either you had no purpose
Or the purpose is beyond the end you figured
And is altered in fulfilment. There are other places
Which also are the world's end, some at the sea jaws,
Or over a dark lake, in a desert or a city –
But this is the nearest, in place and time,
Now and in England.

          If you came this way,
Taking any route, starting from anywhere,
At any time or at any season,
It would always be the same: you would have to put off
Sense and notion. You are not here to verify,
Instruct yourself, or inform curiosity
Or carry report. You are here to kneel
Where prayer has been valid . . .

With the drawing of this Love and the voice of this Calling

We shall not cease from exploration
And the end of all our exploring
Will be to arrive where we started
And know the place for the first time.
Through the unknown, remembered gate
When the last of earth left to discover
Is that which was the beginning;
At the source of the longest river
The voice of the hidden waterfall
And the children in the apple-tree
Not known, because not looked for
But heard, half-heard, in the stillness
Between two waves of the sea.
Quick now, here, now, always –

A condition of complete simplicity
(Costing not less than everything)
And all shall be well and
All manner of thing shall be well
When the tongues of flame are in-folded
Into the crowned knot of fire
And the fire and the rose are one.   *Four Quartets*

Arnold Toynbee
1889–1975

*Toynbee's major survey of the growth and decline of civilisations –
published as the ten-volume* A Study of History *– led him to conclude
that Western European society was on the decline. The solution he
proposed was the development of a universal religion.*

A human being may believe sincerely that he has no religion
but in moments of crisis his religion will assert itself. When
he is confronted with his own imminent death, or when he is
afflicted with bereavement, disappointment, self-reproach or
any other form of acute spiritual suffering, he will find himself
living, even if only for a moment, on the spiritual plane which
he has tried to dismiss as illusion. I therefore feel certain that
there is a future for religious belief. So for me, the question
is: What kind of religion is likely to prevail in the future for
so far as we can see ahead?

Article in *The Listener*

Christianity's fundamental tenet is, as I see it, a belief that
self-sacrificing love is both the best and the most powerful of
all the spiritual impulses that are known to us. I believe that
this is true, and I also believe that the grasp of this truth is
the essence of Christianity; but my holding of this essential
Christian belief does not make me a Christian; for Christianity
is the religion of the Christian Church, and the Church is an
institution.

Experiences

Leslie Weatherhead
1893–1975

It was an appreciation of people's problems, their doubts and, more particularly, their lack of time which made Leslie Weatherhead's ministry so distinctive. He was preacher and pastor at the Congregationalist City Temple in London for nearly thirty years and built up a reputation as a sympathetic counsellor through his public speaking and his broadcasting. His prayer card 'Ten Minutes a Day' and his book A Private House of Prayer *were used by thousands who might otherwise have had no prayer life at all.*

I will tell you about my house of prayer . . . It is easy to memorise the names of the rooms, and you can enter any or all of them as you sit in the corner of a railway carriage, or in the bus or Underground on the way to work, or between your home and the station, or even without getting out of bed . . . Do not rush through all the rooms looking for God. He can be found in every one . . . There are seven rooms in the house and they are all prayer rooms. Here they are, then:

ROOM 1. This is the room in which we *Affirm the Presence of God* . . . All through the Bible God asserts His Presence with His people, and it is real prayer to remember the sentences which recall this to our mind . . . Our Lord not only promised, 'Lo I am with you every day until the end of the world,' but promised the Holy Spirit 'that He may be with you for ever'. In this first room I repeat those great words, 'with you'.

ROOM 2. When we have asserted the fact of the Presence of God, we can pass into the next room in which we *Praise, Thank and Adore God*. It is a good thing to imagine this room full of morning sunshine, for this is the room of thanksgiving. Each of us has something for which to praise and thank God. Indeed it is a revealing thing to write down a list of those things for which we should thank God. We should adore Him for all He is in Himself – and, as we do so, we should call to mind His attributes and remember His love, His splendour, His power, His beauty, His wisdom, His holiness. Then we can thank Him for the way He has led us and for all He has done for us.

ROOM 3. Now we are ready for a room, rather dim and shadowy as we enter, but brighter as we move across it to the window. It is the room of *Confession, Forgiveness and Unloading*. Here we confess our sin, not just in a general way but really being honest . . . In this room part of Psalm 51 would be a suitable piece of furniture; the Psalm in which David pours out his soul to God and finds pardon. Before we leave this room, too, we must make sure that we are ready to forgive others who may have sinned against us . . . Here also we confess our fears and put down our worries and our dark anxieties . . . Our confusion we put down here, too; our bewilderment as to what we ought to do and which way we ought to go. In this room we tell God everything that troubles us.

ROOM 4 is set aside for *Affirmation and Reception*. Cleansed by forgiveness we are ready now to receive . . . The twenty-third Psalm is suitable furniture for this room. It does not ask, 'O Lord, be my Shepherd.' It affirms that He is. It does not ask for guidance. It rests in the affirmation that the soul is being guided. 'He is leading me in a true path for His name's sake and He is restoring my soul.' One should say the words quietly and confidently, repeating each sentence over and over again. Some may wish to visit this room just before sleeping at night. I can think of no more valuable way of falling asleep than to do so repeating some great affirmation about God, such as, 'I will be quiet, resting in Thee, Thou Spirit of Peace within me.'

ROOM 5 is the place for *Purified Desire and Sincere Petition*. We all know what our dominant desires are. In this room we purify them by looking at them again in the light of God . . . We stop saying, 'Give me,' and start saying, 'Make me' and 'Show me' and 'Use me'. This is the place where we ask for renewed trust and stronger faith and more tolerant love for those who differ from us.

ROOM 6 is that of *Intercession for Others*. It has never seemed practicable to me to spend a lot of time on each person for whom I wish to pray, and if the other rooms in the house of prayer have been conscientiously visited, it seems enough to me to say the name of the person slowly, calling him to mind in as vivid a picture as possible, and then imaginatively *watching him emerging from his difficulties*.

ROOM 7 is a big room at the top of the house set aside for *Meditation*. Here we sometimes take an incident in the Gospels and try to do what Ruskin said he did, 'to be present as if in the body at each recorded act in the life of the Redeemer'. We might indeed work steadily through the Gospels in this way, imaginatively watching the incidents happen and especially 'looking at Jesus'.

One could, of course, fill the scheme out to last an hour or more, or shorten it to a few minutes. It is really rather fun to gather passages from the Bible, the hymn book, the poets and the essayists and biographers to make more pictures and furniture for each room. One could in time change the pictures and the furniture in every room . . .

Let us, then, make a house of prayer and, if possible, open the door every morning, for to commune with Him may well be the cause for which we were created.

A Private House of Prayer

C. S. Lewis
1898–1963

C. S. Lewis has been the most popular religious writer in England this century. His achievement was to make Christianity seem sensible again in an age which was trying to dismiss it. The Christian ethic was threaded through all his work, which, besides the more straightforward religious books, included science fiction and the classic 'Narnia' children's series.

My Dear Wormwood,

Obviously you are making excellent progress . . . I am almost glad to hear that he [the 'patient'] is still a churchgoer and a communicant. I know there are dangers in this; but anything is better than that he should realise the break he has made with the first months of his Christian life . . .

A few weeks ago you had to *tempt* him to unreality and inattention in his prayers; but now you will find him opening his arms to you and almost begging you to distract his purpose and benumb his heart. He will *want* his prayers to be unreal, for he will dread nothing so much as effective contact with the Enemy. His aim will be to let sleeping worms lie.

As this condition becomes more fully established, you will be gradually freed from the tiresome business of providing pleasures as temptations . . . You will find that anything or nothing is sufficient to attract his wandering attention. You no longer need a good book, which he really likes, to keep him from his prayers or his work or his sleep; a column of advertisements in yesterday's paper will do. All the healthy and outgoing activities which we want him to avoid can be inhibited and *nothing* given in return, so that at last he may say, as one of my own patients said on his arrival down here, 'I now see that I spent most of my life in doing *neither* what I ought *nor* what I liked.'

Don't forget to use the 'heads I win, tails you lose' argument. If the thing he prays for doesn't happen, then that is one more proof that petitionary prayers don't work; if it does happen, he will, of course, be able to see some of the physical causes which led up to it and 'therefore it would have happened anyway', and thus a granted prayer becomes just as good a proof as a denied one that prayers are ineffective.

The Screwtape Letters (Letters from a senior to a junior devil)

Now the disquieting thing is not simply that we skimp and begrudge the duty of prayer. The really disquieting thing is that it should have to be numbered among duties at all. For we believe that we were created 'to glorify God and enjoy Him forever'. And if the few, very few, minutes we now spend on intercourse with God are a burden to us rather than a delight, what then? If I were a Calvinist this symptom would fill me with despair. What can be done *for* – or what should be done *with* – a rose tree that *dislikes* producing roses? Surely it ought to want to? . . .

If we were perfected, prayer would not be a duty, it would be delight. Some day, please God, it will be. The same is true of many other behaviours which now appear as duties. If I loved my neighbour as myself, most of the actions which are now my moral duty would flow out of me as spontaneously as song from a lark or a fragrance from a flower. Why is this not so yet? . . . The very activities for which we were created are, while we live on earth, variously impeded: by evil in ourselves or in others. Not to practise them is to abandon our humanity. To practise them spontaneously and delightfully is not yet possible. This situation creates the category of duty, the whole specifically *moral* realm . . .

I must say my prayers today whether I feel devout or not; but that is only as I must learn my grammar if I am ever to read the poets.

Letters to Malcolm

Just as the Christian has his moments when the clamour of this visible and audible world is so persistent and the whisper of the spiritual world so faint that faith and reason can hardly stick to their guns, so, as I well remember, the atheist too has his moments of shuddering misgiving, of an all but irresistible suspicion that old tales may after all be true, that something or someone from outside may at any moment break into his neat, explicable, mechanical universe. Believe in God and you will have to face hours when it seems *obvious* that this material world is the only reality; disbelieve in Him and you must face hours when this material world seems to shout at you that it is *not* all. No conviction, religious or irreligious, will, of itself, end once and for all this fifth-columnist in the soul. Only the practice of faith resulting in the habit of faith will gradually do that.

'Religion: Reality or Substitute?'
(essay in *Christian Reflections*)

The terrible thing, the almost impossible thing, is to hand over your whole self – all your wishes and precautions – to Christ. But it is far easier than what we are all trying to do instead. For what we are trying to do is to remain what we call 'ourselves', to keep personal happiness as our great aim in life, and yet at the same time to be 'good'. We are all trying to let our mind and heart go their own way – centred on money or pleasure or ambition – and hoping, in spite of this, to behave honestly and chastely and humbly.

And that is exactly what Christ warned us you could not do. As He said, a thistle cannot produce figs. If I am a field that contains nothing but grass-seed, I cannot produce wheat. Cutting the grass may keep it short: but I shall still produce grass and no wheat. If I want to produce wheat, the change must go deeper than the surface. I must be ploughed up and re-sown.

Do not waste time bothering whether you 'love' your neighbour; act as if you did. As soon as we do this we find one of the great secrets. When you are behaving as if you loved someone, you will presently come to love him. If you injure someone you dislike, you will find yourself disliking him more. If you do him a good turn, you will find yourself disliking him less.

Mere Christianity

217

Stevie Smith
1902–1971

Stevie Smith (christened Florence) spent most of her life living with an aunt in Palmers Green, North London. Such a seemingly dull existence contrasts markedly with her vivid and witty verse.

Scorpion

'This night shall thy soul be required of thee'
My soul is never required of *me*
It always has to be somebody else of course
Will my soul be required of me tonight perhaps?

(I often wonder what it will be like
To have one's soul required of one
But all I can think of is the Out-Patients' Department –
'Are you Mrs Briggs, dear?'
No, I am Scorpion.)

I should like my soul to be required of me, so as
To waft over grass till it comes to the blue sea
I am very fond of grass, I always have been, but there must
Be no cow, person or house to be seen.

Sea and *grass* must be quite empty
Other souls can find somewhere *else*.

O Lord God please come
And require the soul of thy Scorpion

Scorpion so wishes to be gone.

God Speaks

I made Man with too many faults. Yet I love him
And if he wishes, I have a home above for him.
I should like him to be happy. I am genial.
He should not paint me as if I were abominable.
As for instance, that I had a son and gave him for their
    salvation.
This is one of the faults I meant. It leads to nervous
    prostration.

218

All the same, there is a difficulty. I should like him to be
    happy in heaven here,
But he cannot come by wishing. Only by being already at
    home here.

The Airy Christ
(After reading Dr Rieu's translation of St Mark's Gospel)

Who is this that comes in grandeur, coming from the blazing
    East?
This is he we had not thought of, this is he the airy Christ.

Airy, in an airy manner in an airy parkland walking,
Others take him by the hand, lead him, do the talking.

But the Form, the airy One, frowns an airy frown,
What they say he knows must be, but he looks aloofly down,

Looks aloofly at his feet, looks aloofly at his hands,
Knows they must, as prophets say, nailed be to wooden
    bands.

As he knows the words he sings, that he sings so happily
Must be changed to working laws, yet sings he ceaselessly.

Those who truly hear the voice, the words, the happy song,
Never shall need working laws to keep from doing wrong.

Deaf men will pretend sometimes they hear the song, the
    words,
And make excuse to sin extremely; this will be absurd.

Heed it not. Whatever foolish men may do the song is cried
For those who hear, and the sweet singer does not care that
    he was crucified.

For he does not wish that men should love him more than
    anything
Because he died; he only wishes they would hear him sing.

Gerald Vann
1906–1963

Gerald Vann was almost literally a life-long Dominican, first attending the Dominican school in Staffordshire and then joining the Order when he was seventeen. He was ordained in 1929 and became first a teacher, then headmaster at the Dominican school in Northamptonshire. During the 1930s he was a prominent pacifist. He was a popular writer, broadcaster and lecturer and made frequent preaching visits to the United States.

Every human being is unique. It follows that every human being has some unique gift to give to his family: to his parents and brothers and sisters in the ordinary narrow sense, first of all, and thence to his country and to the world. The small world of the human home is built up of the gifts of each member of it; the larger world without is built up in the same way of the various gifts, economic, political, cultural, religious, of the individual citizens. If we are christians we dismiss once and for all the idea that our business in the world is to serve ourselves and nobody else, to become holy ourselves and pay no attention to anyone else . . . Live your life in the unity of the home first of all: train yourself to think in terms of what will make the home a better and a happier place; and then in your building up of the home think of the needs and well-being of your immediate neighbours, and thence of your country and of the whole world; and so you will necessarily live a life of love, and fulfil that much at least – and it is a great deal – of the law of God.

It is important to remind ourselves often that the cultivation of a right sense of humour can be one of the forms of piety. Cultivate a sense of humour in yourself about other people, and in other people about yourself: learn to laugh rather than be vexed by other people's foibles, but learn the ability also to let other people laugh at your own.

The Divine Pity

John Betjeman
1906–1984

By far the most popular and widely-read English poet of the twentieth century, his verse combines ironic wit and social observation with a troubled religious commitment. He loved the Church of England, with all her eccentricities, and was devoted to her church buildings which inspired many of his finest poems.

A Lincolnshire Church

Greyly tremendous the thunder
Hung over the width of the wold
But here the green marsh was alight
In a huge cloud cavern of gold,
And there, on a gentle eminence,
Topping some ash trees, a tower
Silver and brown in the sunlight,
Worn by sea-wind and shower,
Lincolnshire Middle Pointed.
And around it, turning their backs,
The usual sprinkle of villas;
The usual woman in slacks,
Cigarette in her mouth,
Regretting Americans, stands
As a wireless croons in the kitchen
Manicuring her hands.
Dear old, bloody old England
Of telegraph poles and tin,
Seemingly so indifferent
And with so little soul to win.
What sort of church, I wonder?
The path is a grassy mat,
And grass is drowning the headstones
Sloping this way and that.
'Cathedral Glass' in the windows,
A roof of unsuitable slate –
Restored with a vengeance, for certain,
About eighteen-eighty-eight.

The door swung easily open
(Unlocked, for these parts, is odd)
And there on the South aisle altar
Is the tabernacle of God.
There where the white light flickers
By the white and silver veil,
A wafer dipped in a wine-drop
Is the Presence the angels hail,
Is God who created the Heavens
And the wide green marsh as well
Who sings in the sky with the skylark
Who calls in the evening bell,
Is God who prepared His coming
With fruit of the earth for His food
With stone for building His churches
And trees for making His rood.
There where the white light flickers,
Our Creator is with us yet,
To be worshipped by you and the woman
Of the slacks and the cigarette.

The Parish Church in the Fifteenth Century

Not only does everyone go to church on Sunday and in his
best clothes: the church is used on weekdays too, for it is
impossible to say daily prayers in the little hovels in which
most of the villagers live. School is taught in the porch,
business is carried out by the cross in the market where the
booths are (for there are no shops in the village, only open
stalls as in market squares today). In the nave of the church
on a weekday there are probably people gossiping in some
places, while in others there are people praying. There was
no privacy in the Middle Ages, when even princes dined in
public and their subjects watched them eat. The nave of the
church belonged to the people, and they used it as today we
use a village hall or social club. Our new suburban churches
which are used as dance halls during the week with the
sanctuary partitioned off until Sunday, have something in
common with the medieval church. But there is this difference: in the Middle Ages all sport and pleasure, all plays and

dancing were 'under God'. God was near, hanging on his Cross above the chancel arch, and mystically present in the sacrament in the pyx hanging over the altar beyond. His crucifixion was carved on the preaching cross in the church-yard . . .

Small parish churches were not consciously made beautiful. They were built and decorated for effect, to be better than the church in the next village, to be the best building in the village itself, for it is the House of God, and God become Man – that was the great discovery – offered here upon the altar. All sorts of miraculous stories were invented about Him, and even more about His mother. Because He was Man born of woman, He becomes within the grasp of everyone. Few of the extravagances of German and Spanish late medieval art are found in English represen-tations of the scourging, the crucifixion and the deposition. Jesus is thought of as the baby of the poor people who received the tributes of a king. His mother is the most beautiful woman in the world – and how many lovely, loving faces of Our Lady we may see in the old glass, wall-paintings and statues which survive in England. And she bore a Spotless Son who was God and Judge of all. No wonder she was loved by the pious English . . .

Though for the everyday things of life there were friendly saints who helped, life itself must have been terrifying, a continual rush to escape hell. Our Lord and His Mother were the loving and human part of it; hell was the terrifying part. The Devil was seen . . .

The fear that men felt is expressed in the grotesque carvings over the north walls of churches, and in the corbels and bosses of roofs, and in bench-ends, screens and miserere stalls. Their humour is shown there too. Chiefly in the figure of Our Lady do we see the tenderness and sweetness of this late religion.

The Introduction to *English Parish Churches*

Mother Mary Clare
b. 1907

Mother Mary Clare was for many years the Mother General of The Sisters of the Love of God, an Anglican order set up in 1906 – the first founded specifically for those wishing to lead a contemplative monastic life. They moved to their present home at Fairacres, Oxford, in 1914. The community has a strong ecumenical leaning and the extracts below are from an address originally delivered to a conference of Roman Catholic religious.

The most difficult and most decisive part of prayer is acquiring the ability to listen. To listen, according to the dictionary, is 'attentively to exercise the sense of hearing'. It is not a passive affair, a space when we don't happen to be doing or saying anything and are, therefore, automatically able to listen. It is a conscious, willed action, requiring alertness and vigilance, by which our whole attention is focused and controlled. So it is difficult. And it is decisive because it is the beginning of our entry into a personal relationship with God in which we gradually learn to let go of ourselves and allow the Word of God to speak within us.

The one who truly listens is also the one who truly obeys. If we accept the very serious task of stilling ourselves in order to listen to God we may be required to take action, and the result may be as devastating as the result of our Lady's 'Yes' – which was as a sword piercing her heart.

Listening to God

W. H. Auden
1907–1973

Auden resembles T. S. Eliot in his philosophical, almost technical, approach to spirituality, which was one of his enduring preoccupations from mid-career onwards. He even toned down some earlier Marxist poems during this later Christian phase. 'For the Time Being' was written during World War II and was dedicated to his mother, an Anglo-Catholic, who had died in 1941.

from *'Advent'*

If the muscle can feel repugnance, there is still a false move
    to be made;
If the mind can imagine tomorrow, there is still a defeat to
    remember;
As long as the self can say 'I', it is impossible not to rebel;
As long as there is an accidental virtue, there is a necessary
    vice:
And the garden cannot exist, the miracle cannot occur.

For the garden is the only place there is, but you will not
    find it
Until you have looked for it everywhere and found nowhere
    that is not a desert;
The miracle is the only thing that happens, but to you it
    will not be apparent,
Until all events have been studied and nothing happens that
    you cannot explain;
And life is the destiny you are bound to refuse until you
    have consented to die.

Therefore, see without looking, hear without listening,
    breathe without asking:
The Inevitable is what will seem to happen to you purely
    by chance;
The Real is what will strike you as really absurd;
Unless you are certain you are dreaming, it is certainly a
    dream of your own;
Unless you exclaim – 'There must be some mistake' – you
    must be mistaken.

from *'The Massacre of the Innocents'*

HEROD *(contemplating the damage Christ's birth will do to his well-regulated, rational province):*

. . . Civilisation must be saved even if this means sending for the military, as I suppose it does. How dreary. Why is it that in the end civilisation always has to call in these professional tidiers to whom it is all one whether it be Pythagoras or a homicidal lunatic they are instructed to exterminate. Oh dear, why couldn't this wretched infant be born somewhere else? Why can't people be sensible? I don't want to be horrid. Why can't they see that the notion of a finite God is absurd? Because it is. And suppose, just for the sake of argument, that it isn't, that this story is true, that this child is in some inexplicable manner both God and Man, that he grows up, lives, and dies, without committing a single sin? Would that make life any better? On the contrary it would make it far, far worse. For it could only mean this: that once having shown them how, God would expect every man, whatever his fortune, to lead a sinless life in the flesh and on earth. Then indeed would the human race be plunged into madness and despair. And for me personally at this moment it would mean that God had given me the power to destroy Himself. I refuse to be taken in. He could not play such a horrible practical joke. Why should He dislike me so? I've worked like a slave. Ask anyone you like. I read all official dispatches without skipping. I've taken elocution lessons. I've hardly ever taken bribes. How dare He allow me to decide? I've tried to be good. I brush my teeth every night. I haven't had sex for a month. I object. I'm a liberal. I want everyone to be happy. I wish I had never been born . . .

For the Time Being

H. A. Williams
b. 1919

Harry Williams was first a lecturer at Trinity College, Cambridge and later Dean. It was here he set about his task of humanising academic theology, finding it impossible to preach about any facet of Christian belief unless he had full experience of it himself. In 1969 he joined the Anglican Community of the Resurrection at Mirfield, West Yorkshire.

God is always present and waiting to be discovered now, in the present moment, precisely where we are and in what we are doing. That is what we mean when we say that we live in a sacramental universe. Unfortunately we tend to treat the sacrament of our daily life, broken as it is into dozens of small, uneven bits and pieces, as something which hinders us from finding God when in fact it is the very vehicle of his presence. It is as though we were to complain that the bread and wine at the Holy Communion were obstacles to our approach to God instead of the means to it. If, as they do, the bread and wine on the altar represent all we are and do and suffer, then they show us that all our life in its manifold and often petty detail can become God's real presence with us, that it is in the daily bread of our ordinary common experience that we can discern the radiant body of everlasting life. The many things we have to do, the hundred and one calls on our time and attention, don't get between ourselves and God. On the contrary they are to us in very truth his Body and his Blood.

The Joy of God

The joy which a man finds in his work and which transforms the tears and sweat of it into happiness and delight – that joy is God. The wonder and curiosity which welcomes what is new and regards it not as threatening but enriching life – that wonder and curiosity is God. The confidence which leads us to abandon the shelter of our disguises and to open up the doors of our personality so that others may enter there, and both we and they be richer for the contact – that confidence is God. The vision which enables us to see the majesty of

men, of all men including ourselves, piercing through the
ugliness of the obscuring pathology to the beauty of the real
person – that power of vision is God. The sense of belonging
to the natural world, the exhilarating certainty that all things
are ours whether things in heaven or things on the earth –
that sense of belonging is God. The superabundance which
leads us naturally and inevitably to give, not as a matter of
duty nor in a spirit of patronage, but because we cannot
forbear – that superabundance is God. The compelling
conviction that in spite of all evidence to the contrary, in spite
of all the suffering we may have to witness or to undergo, the
universe is on our side, and works not for our destruction but
for our fulfilment – that compelling conviction is God.

When Jesus urged men to repent, he was urging them to
become as little children. He wasn't asking them to eat the
dust. He was confronting them with the necessity of a radical
change of outlook, a fundamental re-orientation of their lives,
so that they would no longer trust for security in the persons
they had built up – the drama of being me which I continu-
ously stage for my own benefit – so that they would no longer
trust that, but have the courage to become as receptive as
little children, with all the openness to life, the taking down
of the shutters and the throwing away of the armour which
that entails . . .

That is what repentance means: discovering that you have
more to you than you dreamt or knew, becoming bored with
being only a quarter of what you are and therefore taking the
risk of surrendering to the whole, and thus finding more
abundant life . . .

It's obvious how important repentance is for the Christian.
It was part of the basic message of Jesus. He began his
ministry by telling men to repent and believe in the gospel.
Unless, therefore, we are willing to repent, we cannot be his
disciples.

The True Wilderness

Because of the communion of saints, the mystery of the Body
of Christ, because we are all very closely inter-related, therefore none of us can enter into the presence of God simply for

himself alone. However and whenever we pray and whatever the form of our prayers, our communion with God always flows out from us to mankind. But since mankind as a whole is far too large a concept for our limited imagination, we can't pray with much meaning for all men everywhere. We have to particularise, praying for particular people or peoples, those we love or those in need, individuals whose plight has been brought home to us or collectivities like the peoples of Russia or Southern Africa . . .

Real prayer leads to action, leads to us doing what we can for people. But it also saves us from fantasies of omnipotence, of imagining that we can do for people what we manifestly can't do, and from the anxiety and guilt-feelings such fantasies evoke. And praying for people also makes us sensitive to their deepest needs which are generally not their most obvious ones. By means of our prayer God succours people in the very centre and core of their being, and that is what they need most.

Becoming What I Am

So shocked are we at the irreverence and so ashamed of the rational absurdity of letting off our aggressions against God, that we repress them so far as God is concerned and appear to ourselves not to feel them. And then we wonder why, after we have prayed so devoutly, we feel so bloody-minded towards poor inoffensive John Smith or sweet little helpful Mary Jones or, more often, the members of our own family. Your wife, you see, has very often to have thrown at her the rotten eggs you really want to throw at God. And the joke is that God is not in the slightest degree taken in by the pantomine by which you deceive yourself. He knows what we won't admit to ourselves, that the rotten eggs are really meant for him.

When we experience God as a meeting with another to whom we are closely linked as to a father or a friend, then the ambivalence of our feelings is inevitable. It is far better to accept that fact honestly and admit it to ourselves than to repress it. There is great wisdom in Mrs Patrick Campbell's warning not to do it in the street and frighten the horses. But that prudent condition observed, if you want to blaspheme, then for Christ's sake blaspheme. If you want in your prayers to grouse, then for Christ's sake grouse. If you hate God, then for Christ's sake tell him you do and tell him why. He will know that these things are the necessary obverse of your love for him and that he is himself responsible for having made you that way. By having the courage of your aggression you will show greater trust in him and greater love for him than by all that 'resigned submissive meek' stuff which leaves you to take the hell out of other people, and not least out of yourself so that in consequence there is far less of you to give away.

In the New Testament the cross is more than once described as a conflict, as a creative conflict which leads to resurrection. The vocation of being human is a vocation to enter into that creative conflict and make it our own. It is true that to each individual person the call to conflict will come in a particular way. But behind that particular call is the general one to recognize and accept and welcome the life-giving cross in each and every department of our lives.

Tensions

Ruth Burrows
b. 1929

A Carmelite nun living near Norwich, Sister Ruth Burrows has shown in her autobiography that the life of a full-time 'religious' is not packed with mystical visions and divine communications. 'From my earliest childhood,' she writes, 'God has hidden himself from me and hides himself still'; though she can add, 'Now I am happy that this is so.'

It is impossible to understand my life unless it is seen all the time against the background of black depression . . . The heart of this seems to have been fear, fear not of this or that precisely, but an ultimate fear, fear of my relation to God. Unless one has security in the Absolute; unless there is ground to being and ground to my own being then any assurances, any 'security', is mocked. To enjoy anything is mockery . . .

230

If only God would give me one touch of his love so that I could really feel that he loved me! I prayed for this but found myself adding: 'only if it pleases you'. I could not pray for favours in prayer. All I wanted was love. I wanted to love God and I would only want what would enable me to love him. I began to realise that it might be God's plan that I should always bear this desolation. Over and over again I would tell him that I was ready to do so provided it would lead to greater love. Never did I think I had deserved any favour but I knew that God does not give according to deserts.

The year before my final profession, James [Ruth's brother] married and brought his bride to see me on the evening of the wedding. I was deeply moved to see him so changed, to see their radiant happiness. I thought of them going off together, to the intimacy of their first night. No sooner had they left the parlour than I burst into a fit of weeping. My own lot seemed so utterly bitter. Nothing, nothing, nothing, bleak, cheerless, lonely. And I found myself turning in the darkness to God, telling him I would go on to the end of my days feeling loveless if it pleased him. Truly there was a citadel within held by the living God.

As a little one, preparing for confession, I was conscious of a sort of acting. I had to draw up a list of sins with the number of times. I think I can say with certainty that in my mind I did not in any way relate the items of this list to God, even though I called them sins.

Lately I have come to realise that my notion of sin has been too limited. I thought of sin as a deliberate offence against God, a partial or total rejection of him. Of this I could not consider a child capable and I would even question if anyone is capable of it. Are we big enough? But now I see that it is a mistake to restrict sin to specific and somewhat outstanding acts, as though the rest of our acts (and inactivity is act) when not God-centred are neutral. Rather is sin to be seen as an orientation, a more or less continual series of choices against what one knows in one's deepest heart is right. It is an evasion of life, a refusal to stand in the truth of one's being. This is the offence to God, that his beloved creatures, to whom he longs to give himself, refuse this gift. This gift of

231

his love is enshrined in the acceptance of ourselves and in life as it really is . . . 'My life is in my hands'; this is true of each of us. I can treasure every drop of my life or I can squander it, letting it drip through my fingers as something of no account.

Before the Living God

Acknowledgements

The compilers are most grateful for permission to use copyright material by the following authors. Where a title is not given, full details will be found in the text.

Aelred: reprinted from the translation by Geoffrey Webb and Adrian Walker (Mowbrays, 1962) by permission of A. R. Mowbray & Co. Ltd.

Anselm: this version © Little Gidding Books.

W. H. Auden: the two pieces, both from *For the Time Being*, reprinted from *Collected Poems* by permission of Faber and Faber Ltd.

Bede: the two lyrics reprinted from *A Choice of Anglo-Saxon Verse* by permission of the translator, Richard Hamer, and Faber and Faber Ltd; the prose reprinted from *A History of the English Church and People* translated by Leo Sherley-Price (Penguin Classics 1955, 1968) by permission of Penguin Books Ltd.

John Betjeman: 'A Lincolnshire Church' reprinted from *Collected Poems* by permission of John Murray (Publishers) Ltd; the prose passage reprinted from *The Collins Guide to English Parish Churches* by permission of William Collins Sons & Co. Ltd.

Catherine Bramwell-Booth: reprinted by permission of Lion Publishing.

Anna Bunston: 'Under a Wiltshire Apple Tree' from *Collected Poems* reprinted by permission of The Mitre Press.

Ruth Burrows: reprinted by permission of Sheed and Ward Ltd.

Caedmon: reprinted from *A Choice of Anglo-Saxon Verse* by permission of the translator, Richard Hamer, and Faber and Faber Ltd.

Cloud of Unknowing: this version © Little Gidding Books.

Cuthbert: reprinted from Helen Waddell's translation, *Beasts and Saints* by permission of Constable & Co. Ltd.

Dream of the Rood: reprinted from *A Choice of Anglo-Saxon Verse* by permission of the translator, Richard Hamer, and Faber and Faber Ltd.

King Edmund: material from *Suffolk Scene* by Julian Tennyson reprinted by permission of Blackie and Son Ltd.

T. S. Eliot: extracts from *Four Quartets* reprinted by permission of Mrs Valerie Eliot and Faber and Faber Ltd.

Everyman: reprinted from *Everyman and Other Medieval Mystery Plays* edited by A. C. Cawley (Everyman's Library) by permission of J. M. Dent & Sons.

Godric: reprinted from Helen Waddell's translation, *Beasts and Saints* by permission of Constable & Co. Ltd.

Walter Hilton: this version © Little Gidding Books.

Julian of Norwich: this version © Little Gidding Books.

Margery Kempe: reprinted from *The Book of Margery Kempe* edited by W. Butler-Bowden (World Classics edition, 1954) by permission of Oxford University Press.

William Langland: this version © Little Gidding Books.

C. S. Lewis: reprinted by permission of William Collins Sons & Co. Ltd.

Rose Macaulay: material from *Letters to a Friend* (Collins) reprinted by permission of A. D. Peters & Co. Ltd.; material from *The Towers of Trebizond* reprinted by permission of William Collins Sons & Co. Ltd.

Mother Mary Clare: extracts from Fairacres Publication 69 reprinted by permission of SLG Press.

Pearl: this version © Little Gidding Books.

Riddle: reprinted from *A Choice of Anglo-Saxon Verse* by permission of the translator, Richard Hamer, and Faber and Faber Ltd.

Richard Rolle: this version © Little Gidding Books.

Stevie Smith: the three poems reprinted from *The Collected Poems of Stevie Smith* (Penguin Modern Classics) by permission of James MacGibbon, executor.

William Temple: reprinted by permission of Macmillan, London and Basingstoke.

Arnold Toynbee: material from *Experiences* (Oxford University Press, 1969) reprinted by permission of OUP.

Evelyn Underhill: material from *Collected Papers of Meditations and Prayers* reprinted by permission of Longman; material from *The Essentials of Mysticism* and *The Golden Sequence* reprinted by permission of the copyright holders, the Evelyn Underhill Charitable Trust.

Leslie Weatherhead: material from *A Private House of Prayer* (published by Arthur James) reprinted by permission of Edward England Books.

Gerald Vann: reprinted by permission of William Collins Sons & Co. Ltd.

H. A. Williams: material from *Tensions* and *The Joy of God* reprinted by permission of Mitchell Beazley; material from *The True Wilderness* reprinted by permission of Constable & Co. Ltd.

Virginia Woolf: reprinted by permission of Quentin Bell and Angelica Garnett and The Hogarth Press.

In addition, the Editors would like to thank all the members of the community at Little Gidding who have helped with the compiling of this anthology, and in particular Hazel Rowbottom, Ann Tilley, Margaret Smith and Anna Saunders. Thanks also to Sister Pia of the Institute of the Blessed Virgin Mary in Cambridge and to Howard Coutts, formerly of the Victoria and Albert Museum, for their advice.

Index of Authors